UNSTOPPABLE RETURNS IN A BEAR MARKET

5 SECRET INVESTING STRATEGIES TO BEAT THE STOCK MARKET AND MAXIMIZE RETURNS IN A RECESSION

CORNS ELBA

© Copyright 2022 - Cornelis Elba All rights reserved.

It is not legal to reproduce, duplicate, or transmit any part of this document in either electronic means or printed format. Recording of this publication is strictly prohibited and any storage of this document is not allowed unless with written permission from the publisher, except for the use of brief quotations in a book review.

Disclaimer

The financial topics discussed in this book are for educational purposes only. Past performance is no guarantee of future returns. No investment performance is guaranteed or implied.

CONTENTS

About the Author	vii
Introduction	ix
1. BEAR: BOON OR BANE?	1
Understanding economic cycles	2
The "bear" facts	4
There are typically four stages to a bear market.	10
Important facts about bears	12
Chapter Takeaways	15
2. RELAX AND PLAY ALONG	17
Surviving the bear timeline	18
How bears affect your brain	25
Avoid acting on your emotions	30
Avoid acting on the "wisdom" of the crowd	39
Chapter Summary	41
3. WHAT TIME IS BETTER FOR INVESTING?	43
Failures of market timing	48
Time *in*, not tim-*ing*	51
What goes wrong when you wait too long	53
Chapter Summary	55
4. DOLLAR-COST AVERAGING IS YOUR ALLY	57
What is DCA and when is the best time to use it?	57
Dollar-cost averaging in a bear market	63
Sample DCA in a steeply declining market	71
How you can start using dollar-cost averaging to your advantage	73
Chapter Summary	76

5. DIVERSIFY WITHOUT DISENGAGING 77
   The necessities of diversification in a down
   market 80
   Play defensive 82
   Grow in a bear 86
   Deal with dividends 93
   Don't forget your bonds 98
   Chapter Summary 106

6. GET SHORT-Y 107
   Short-selling in a bear 108
   Put options 121
   ETFs for bears 126
   Chapter Summary 136

7. PREPPING YOUR BEAR ATTACK TOOLKIT 139
   The right mindset is your ally 140
   Practice good hygiene for your portfolio 144
   Prior proper planning (helps) prevent poor
   performance 148
   Chapter Summary 150

   Conclusion 153
   Bibliography 157

A SPECIAL GIFT FOR YOU

A FREE GIFT TO OUR READERS

Are your investment funds underperforming the markets? I share with you four proven steps to manage your fund wealth in a recession.

Diversification through mutual or exchange-traded funds is not enough to protect your portfolio in bear markets and recession conditions.

What if your diversified funds are still performing poorly, how do you know when it's time to ditch your fund or stick along with them? I share with your four practical steps to test on your portfolio TODAY. You can download and start using now!

Scan the QR code below to access your free gift:

https://bit.ly/3DjXQ8D

ABOUT THE AUTHOR

Corns Elba is a passionate and dedicated investor with over ten years of experience. He believes that investing is a skill that most people should be aware of as investors play a vital role in the growth and success of a company. In addition, he believes that stock market investing can provide fortunes for investors and a path to financial freedom.

He loves to provide and educate people through his educative content published across various social media platforms. He wishes to illuminate his audience with his experiences and the risks and opportunities on investing. So his purpose is to upskill individuals' knowledge by providing them with essential information and insights to empower on investment decisions.

After witnessing multiple stock market crashes, Corns believes they present plenty of longer-term opportunities. So he got to grips with unleashing his intellect and experience by penning his thoughts down. He plans on pursuing his writing career by publishing a series of books on investing and covering different aspects and strategies to maximize return.

He aims to craft books that are ideal for novices and savvy investors, providing in-depth information on new perspectives and insights, making them classic and exciting guides for those planning to invest and making intelligent investment choices.

INTRODUCTION

"For those properly prepared, the bear market is not a calamity but an opportunity."

— JOHN TEMPLETON

Many investors believe that a 20% downturn in stock prices – which is the official definition of a bear market – is a calamity that stops their investment plans in their tracks. But smarter investors know better. In each of the 11 bear markets that have occurred since World War II, the year after that 20% decline results in an average 12.4% gain, compared to the usual average of 7.5%.[1]

It's not always easy to stay invested when you see the value of the index or your portfolio dropping. If you invest $1,000 and there's a 20% drop, your money is now only worth $800. But as long as you don't make that loss real, by selling your investment after it drops, then you'll capture the rebound when the market goes back up, as it always has so far.

No one knows when the next bear market will hit, though often there are signs that point to a potential stock drop in the offing. On the other hand, sometimes these signals turn out to really just be noise. You'll discover how to deal with a declining market in a way that won't hamper your investing if the bear market doesn't appear, or only hangs on for a day or two.

Bear markets will end. Even if it seems like the stock market drop doesn't seem to be getting any better, it will. The smart money knows how to take advantage of the stock drop – and with this book, you're now "smart money".

You'll learn the techniques that others have used not just to stay afloat when the market's down, but to take the decline and use it to your advantage. This type of financial information isn't taught in schools, so don't feel bad if this is all new to you. The important thing is that you recognize that you can make money no matter how the stock market happens to be performing.

You may have been investing in the last recession, but without these tools, you may have ended up with actual losses instead of paper ones. Now you'll learn how to equip yourself so you don't have to make the same mistakes. Once you've read through this book, you'll have a solid toolbox to work with.

No more diving down the rabbit hole of the Internet chasing down bear market strategies that may or may not work, or that someone may be paid to talk about. There are a lot of people giving stock advice online who aren't qualified or are being paid to shill certain products or both. There are also qualified people, but they're scattered among different websites and forums, so they're hard to keep track of.

Right now you might be wondering why you should read my book. I'm not being paid by any company to discuss the topics in this book, nor about the investments I'll mention in later chapters. I think more hardworking people should keep more of their hard-earned money, and so I've written this book to spread the message to as many people as I can.

There's money to be made in a bear just as there is in a bull, but not that many people talk about that, or the specific strategies that you can use. I'm an investor with over 15 years of experience in both bull and bear markets. I know what works and what doesn't from my own investments and from all the global research I've done during this time.

By reading this book and understanding how investments work in a bear market, you'll find a number of benefits. You'll discover strategies that aren't covered by many other authors, such as shorting and how to diversify in a bear market specifically.

- Learn to control your feelings

Emotions are often a problem for investors. Fear and greed are major motivators for purchases (ask any advertising executive). When prices are rising, investors get greedy. After all, everyone else is making money, so why shouldn't they? But when the pendulum swings as it always does, investors who see the value of their investments dropping give in to fear. They buy high and sell low, which is how people lose money.

Instead, you'll learn to view the market in a rational and logical way. Whether the market is rising or falling simply means that you have different opportunities for making money. You learn to evaluate your investments from a strategic perspective, instead of making decisions driven by market sentiment.

- Buy low

Imagine that you're going shopping for shoes. How do you feel when you see a "Sale" sign at the entrance to the shoe department? Wonderful—because you know you're getting a bargain. Same with clothing, cars, and anything else: buying on sale means that you pay less for the same item.

Bear markets are the same with stocks. These investments are now on sale, and the wise shopper will scoop them up at a lower price when they can.

- Understand your risk tolerance

It's easy to be aggressive and take more risks when things are going your way. It's the downside that really helps you understand how risk-averse you might be. Then you'll know what you can handle going forward. You may have more of an appetite for risk than you thought, so you can invest in something that has big upside potential.

Or you may find it hard to sleep at night when your investments have dropped below a certain level, so you need to take a little less risk with your investments. Remember, risk and reward are two sides of the same coin. No risk, no reward.

- Be more consistent

It's critical to stay invested in the stock market, even when things look bleak. No one has a crystal ball to know when the tide will turn, and if you sell out of fear, you won't be able to get back in time to be invested during the days when the market soars. Staying in through thick and thin is how you'll benefit from those big gains.

On the other hand, you only get these benefits when you apply them during a market decline! You've got to seize the opportunities while you can, or they go away once the market begins to rise again.

It's pretty easy to fall down Internet rabbit holes, hoping that you'll come across some good strategies for staying alive in a bear market. Or you can read this book to find the five techniques that will help you make money during a stock market decline. So what are you waiting for? The sooner you read through this, the quicker you can start using these tools for your own benefit. So let's take that bear by the horns!

1

BEAR: BOON OR BANE?

> "There is nothing either good or bad but thinking makes it so."
>
> — HAMLET (FROM *HAMLET* BY WILLIAM SHAKESPEARE, ACT II, SCENE II)

Maybe Shakespeare's Hamlet didn't have to deal with the stock market, but the mindset you have about a bear market determines whether or not you'll be able to seize its opportunities. Understanding the economic cycles and how they work can also help you look at a bear market more objectively. It's also important to be able to spot some of the signals of a bear in order to prepare.

UNDERSTANDING ECONOMIC CYCLES

Just as the market cycles between bulls (rising in value) and bears (dropping in value), the economy as a whole cycles between contraction (recession) and expansion (growth). These periods don't necessarily equal each other in duration or intensity; the US economy grew for about ten years (2009—2019) despite the Great Recession that lasted about two.

Some of the components of growth and contraction include interest rates, total employment, consumer spending, and GDP (gross domestic product). These components don't move in lockstep either; consider the high inflation of over 9% in the first half of 2022 (usually a contraction signal) which coincided with a high employment rate (usually an expansive signal). Historically, inflation is generally 2—3%.

There are four phases of the economic cycle. It's not always clear when one phase begins to shift into another, but these are the general characteristics of each one. On average, a US economic cycle lasts about 5 ½ years, but there's a wide range of variability in that number. [2]

1. Expansion

Here the economy is growing. Production may be increasing, and interest rates tend to be low. That encourages investment, not just in the stock market, but in people, machines, and other aspects of growing companies.

2. Peak

At some point the economy will hit the high point or peak of the cycle. This happens when growth reaches its maximum for that particular cycle (the peak of one economic cycle may not be higher than the previous one.) This will often result in some imbalances in the economy.

3. Contraction

This generally occurs in conjunction with a stock market correction. Growth slows or stagnates, the employment rate starts falling, and prices stop appreciating.

4. Trough

As you've probably guessed, this is the lowest point of the economic cycle. A trough in one cycle is not necessarily the same as one in a different cycle. However, once the economy has hit the trough, there's only one direction for it to go in (eventually) and that direction is up.

You may have heard of different schools of thought as to why the cycles fluctuate and what causes shifts between phases. Because it's not entirely clear which school is right, it's not terribly important to explore them.

As an investor, what you really need to understand are the potential signals that can tell you whether the cycle is ready to move into a new phase or not, and you'll learn about them later on. Before we get there, though, you also need to understand what exactly a bear market is and its potential causes, as well as things to know about them that will help you keep your wits about you when you encounter a bear on Wall Street.

THE "BEAR" FACTS

As you learned earlier, in basic terms, the bear market is marked by a decline of 20% or more from the recent high. It's not just used for the stock market as a whole but can refer to a single stock or other investment that has experienced this type of steep drop.

What is "the market"? Markets are often defined by indices that are made up of a variety of companies. While the S&P 500 is a well-known market index, it represents the 500 largest companies in the US. There are other indices, such as the DJIA (Dow Jones Industrial Average) that represents 30 large, well-known US stocks. NASDAQ typically refers to tech stocks.

Bear markets happen across all different types of companies and therefore many of the indices. The S&P 500 is a well-known index that does a pretty good job of representing US companies as a whole, so you'll see a lot of references to this index throughout the book.

The 20% number for a bear market doesn't actually have any special statistical significance, other than providing a psychological obstacle for investors. That's a large enough drop that some investors might be stopped in their tracks.

Theories abound as to why Wall Street refers to bulls and bears. One hypothesis is that since bears hibernate, a bear market is a market in retreat. Since bulls are known to charge, a bull market signifies expansion. Another is that bulls toss their horns up in the air when they're attacking, which indicates a price rise. Since bears push down with their paws on their prey, they're indicating price drops.

Whatever you might think about why a declining market is referred to as a bear, the critical point is that they're a feature, not a bug, of the stock market. A drop in prices, no matter how steep, is necessary for the market to work. It doesn't mean the end of the world is nigh.

Price declines can take out some of the "froth" if the stock or market has been on a bull run, and also provides investors with a cheaper entry point – provided, of course, that the investors are alert for such opportunities!

The size of the decline separates a bear market from a *market correction*, though you may have seen these two terms used interchangeably elsewhere. A market correction is a drop of at least 10% but it stops short of the 20% mark. To put that into perspective, if you have $1,000 a market correction will drop the value down to $900. But a bear market will drive it to $800, if not lower since bears can drop more than 20%.

Corrections also tend to end more quickly than bears: they may linger for weeks, but a bear can stay around for months or even years. The bear market that accompanied the dot-com crash in the early 2000s lasted 929 days, which is almost 3 years.[3]

Bears are often characterized as *secular* or *cyclical*. A secular bear can be driven by external forces and last for years, whereas the cyclical types are generally a result of the market and tend to last months rather than years.

The major causes of bear markets include:

- Recessions

First, let's define exactly what a recession is. Two-quarters of falling GDP (gross domestic product) meet the definition of a recession. Not all recessions end in bears or vice versa; for example, the Black Monday crash in 1987 didn't result in a bear market even though the S&P 500 tanked that day.

Recessions are typically marked by a loss of consumer and business confidence. Once people begin losing confidence, spending and investing start to dry up. High-interest rates can also tip the economy into recession because it's harder for businesses and consumers to borrow money to invest or spend.

A bear market can also cause a recession, which is a bit of a chicken-or-the-egg situation. Housing prices and sales that start dropping can also influence the slowdown of the economy. Even deregulation can play a part in a recession if important safeguards are removed.

Post-war slowdowns and wage-price controls (last seen in the 1970s) may also cause a recession. Credit crunches and bubbles popping may also send the economy into a downward slide, as can deflation, when prices drop instead of rising over time.

- Public health crisis

The COVID-19 pandemic is an excellent example of a public health crisis that can result in a bear. When fewer people are consuming and engaged in business, the economy suffers as a result.

- Geopolitical crisis

Russia's attack on Ukraine probably contributed to the bear market in May 2022 as well as the tail end of the pandemic. Earlier, the Persian Gulf War in the 1990s contributed to the bear market at that time.

- Popped market bubbles

The subprime housing debacle resulted in the Great Recession of 2008-2009, which as you may recall led to a pretty significant bear market. Likewise, the dot-com bubble as noted above was accompanied by a steep decline.

- Economic slowdown/negative economic data

These often overlap with recessions, but don't always. You can have an economic slowdown without tipping over into an actual recession. The second-longest bear (after the Great Depression) took place in the early 1970s and started slowly. Inflation had increased and the economic news turned negative.

Then the oil cartel OPEC launched an embargo in 1973, which led to the lines of cars outside gas stations that you may have heard of. In 1974 the Watergate scandal resulted in President Nixon's resignation, which just made things worse. However, given these enormous downward pressures, the bear began to retreat towards the end of 1974 and stocks started looking up.

- Monetary/fiscal policies aimed at contraction

These policies are undertaken by the government to manage the economy (as much as it can be managed.) *Monetary* policy is driven by the US central bank, the Federal Reserve (the

"Fed"). It tackles inflation, regulates interest rates, and in general tries to ensure the banking system works smoothly.

Fiscal policy is influenced by the US government's taxing and spending powers, designed to help maintain employment, spur business creation and growth, and support the growth of the economy over the long term.

These two policies can't always work in harmony, and the levers they use are imprecise. A policy aimed at combating inflation by raising interest rates, for example, could fuel a bear market.

THERE ARE TYPICALLY FOUR STAGES TO A BEAR MARKET.

1. Spot the bear

Most investors in the modern world understand that prices fluctuate, and that *volatility* or up and down changes in price are a feature of the stock market. Given that stocks can decline and then rise again, it's not always obvious at first that the market has entered the bear stage. However, eventually, investors who realize that the decline is ready to stick around for a while start selling. (Bad idea.)

2. Panic - it's a bear!

Once more and more investors recognize that the market has officially entered bear territory, some investors start to unload their stock as fast as they can, leading to widespread fear-based selling. (Really bad idea.)

Trading volume will also start declining, because once people have sold out they're afraid to get back in again, and other investors may hold their fire. Typically economic news is also getting worse, and investor sentiment is decidedly negative.

3. Stabilize

Despite the name, this stage is often the most turbulent and volatile of a bear. Here, investors have begun to recognize what's going on and the cause of this particular stock decline. This stage can last the longest. This stage is also often characterized by rallies and reversals, as market speculators enter the game and push prices up briefly before selling again.

4. Find the bear bottom

Here the price declines begin to level off. There may be some good economic data that persuades investors to return, or the prospect of getting more value for the dollar helps jump-start trading again.

IMPORTANT FACTS ABOUT BEARS

Hopefully, by now you're feeling more comfortable about the idea of a bear market. They're an expected phase of the economic cycle, and they have predictable stages that you'll progress through until the decline ends, as you know it will. But there are some additional characteristics of a market in decline that will help you make good decisions once you acquire the tools.

1. Keep your eyes open for the 20% signal

The market cycles discussed earlier are measured from their high points (peaks) to the low points (troughs). Once prices have fallen 20% from the recent peak, a bear market is indicated. (A new bull market begins when prices reach 20% above the recent low.)

2. Average bear losses are lower than average bull gains

Since WWII, bear losses have averaged about 32.7% decline.[4] But the bulls have averaged gains of roughly 112%.[5] So if you stay invested through the bear in order to experience the full bull market afterward you'll come out way ahead.

3. Bears don't live very long

There is a wide variety on the range, but as noted above, the longest was short of three years. On average they're only active for about nine months (289 days).[6]

4. Bears are a feature, not a bug

Since 1928 there have been 26 bear markets, so they're not exactly unheard of. You've learned about some of the benefits of bears, so the good news is that you'll have plenty of opportunities to capitalize on them in your investing career!

5. Bears occur relatively frequently… but not as frequently as before WWII

The average time between bears is 3.6 years – but remember, there are some pretty wide-apart data points. Before World War II, they happened about 1.4 years apart on average; but after the war, it's been more like 5+ years apart. If it's been 3.6 years since the last bear, you don't have to go searching for one if market conditions aren't favorable for a bear.

While we've recently experienced a huge bull run from the end of the Great Recession until 2020 and the pandemic, there was actually a longer one from December 1987 (after Black Monday) that ran until the dot-com bubble burst in March 2000. These two ran uninterrupted by any 20% declines.

In other words, though you can expect periodic bears, they don't happen on a regular cycle. A certain period of years having elapsed will not cause a bear; bad economic data, geopolitical shocks, etc., are the reasons a bear will raise its head. In a 50-year market ride, you'll probably experience about 14 bears.

6. Big positive days happen during bears

This is another key factor in why you should not sell while the bear is running. Rallies happen (that are later squelched), but if you sell at a loss and miss a big positive day, you'll definitely be worse off than if you just rode it out.

Half of the S&P 500 index's biggest days occurred during bear markets, and another 24% happened before the bear was officially recognized.[7] No one knows when these days will happen, so being invested in the market, in general, is the only way to capture them.

7. A bear does not mean a recession is happening

Since 1929 there have been 26 bear markets but "only" 15 recessions. No one enjoys recessions, but they're also an inescapable part of the modern economy. The stock market is a component of the economy, but it doesn't drive the whole thing. A bear doesn't mean that you'll lose your job or experience the other kinds of economic pain that are common during recessions.

8. The market is mostly positive, even though declines are painful

Although investors tend to remember the year 2008, they don't always remember the huge bull run that ran for years afterward. They don't remember the year 2013, in which large company stocks rose over 30% and small and mid-sized companies rose 40-50%. That year saw a US government shutdown, and no one had predicted it would be such a stellar year for stocks.

The reason that the declines are so painful and easy to remember is due to a cognitive bias known as risk aversion. Human brains are wired to feel the pain of loss twice as much as the happiness from an equivalent gain. In other words, losing $100 feels twice as bad as the happiness we get from winning $100 feels. If we didn't have that bias, since the amount is the same, the magnitude of emotion should be the same either positive or negative.

So we tend to remember these bear markets, even though in the past 92 years of investing they've only accounted for about 21 of those years. Most of the time, the stock market is positive.

CHAPTER TAKEAWAYS

Bear markets are regular occurrences in the stock market, and nothing to be afraid of. In fact, you can make money from these periods of lower prices while other investors are losing their heads around you. Just because there's a bear market doesn't mean that the economy will necessarily fall into a recession. Although bear markets may seem to be incredibly painful, they only make up a small amount of your time invested. Understanding the characteristics of a bear market will help you profit from them.

In the next chapter, you'll discover your first tool for benefiting from a 20% market decline: staying cool and knowing how to handle yourself, even if you might be worried or anxious about the bear standing in your investing path.

2

RELAX AND PLAY ALONG

As you've learned, emotions run high for investors, especially when markets are down. But that doesn't mean that you have to let yourself be infected by these fears. Playing along and overriding emotions when it happens will help you make smart decisions and seize opportunities.

In 2002, for example, at the bottom of a 2.5-year bear market, the S&P 500 bounced back 15% in one month and 34% over the next year.[8]

The question becomes, no matter which index you're looking at, how do you stick with your investing plan when it seems like everything (and everyone) is falling apart?

SURVIVING THE BEAR TIMELINE

No matter how painful a 20% or more decline can be, a bear market too will pass. The shortest one happened in 2020 and lasted 33 days—barely a month. There's never been a bear market that didn't hit bottom and then lead to a bull market.

Looking at past bear markets can help you prepare for the next one so that you can take it in your stride. We've talked about how bear markets don't last very long, and if you take out the 2000 and 2020 events (which were the longest and shortest bears, respectively) the average duration is just about one year or 388 days.[9]

It's also important to recognize that just because the stock market has dropped 20%, your portfolio may not. If you've diversified your assets and have some bonds, cash, or other investments that don't fall along with the stock market, your portfolio might decline somewhat less than that.

Although that one year may seem like an eternity if you're not prepared to face it. The better you learn to handle surprises, especially negative ones, in the stock market, the more easily you'll be able to stick to your plan even after a steep drop in prices. The following are some methods you can use to keep your cool.

- Review your risk tolerance and goals

When prices are rising, it's easy to forget how painful a severe drop can be, and it's easy to get caught up in the madness of crowds, especially when it comes to investing. You may have bought into some very risky assets, which are likely to lose value in a bear. Take a look at what you own and see if any of it looks risky or speculative. If so, it may be time to sell.

Likewise, what are your financial goals? They may be different from what you considered in the past, and some time may have gone by. What do your goals and timeframes look like now? You may be able to invest in less risky assets because you've already achieved the growth you needed. Now your goal is to avoid losing it all in the market just when you need the money.

Conversely, maybe you haven't been investing consistently or for some other reason aren't on track to achieve those goals. How much time do you have left? How much more risk can you afford to take?

Risk tolerance is actually composed of two components: your ability to take risks and your aversion to (or embrace of) risk. Your ability depends on your timeframe: if you're less than ten years away from your goal, you can't afford to try to ride out the bear with all your money, so you're not able to take as much risk.

Your aversion to risk is more personal: how you feel when you lose 10%, 15%, or 20% of your portfolio. If you're risk averse, a steep drop will leave you unable to sleep at night.

These two components may not coincide with each other. For example, you could embrace risk and feel no worry when you see your portfolio drop 20% or more. But if your goal is five years away, you don't have the ability to take that much risk.

And on the flip side, maybe even a 10% loss of money will keep you tossing and turning at night. But if your goal is more than ten years from now, you need to take more risks so that you can outrun inflation over that time period. Your ability to take risks is high, but you're personally risk-averse.

- Rebalance your portfolio

Once you've determined what your risk tolerance is, you can figure out how much money to have in bonds and fixed income and what portion to allot to stocks and equity. However, as the market does its thing, your portfolio's allocation will change.

For instance, suppose you have a 60/40 allocation where 60% of your money is in stocks and 40% is in bonds. This balance gives you the long-term compound growth you need in the stock portion, but you can sleep at night because you have enough money that isn't in the stock market and doesn't drop when the stock market does.

After a year of stock market growth, your allocation might have shifted to 65/35. This doesn't seem like a big deal during a bull run, but as soon as stock prices start declining, you'll realize you don't have enough of a bond cushion. A simple way to avoid this is to periodically *rebalance* your portfolio back to its original allocation.

It's simple, but not always easy. In the example above, you'd sell enough stocks and buy enough bonds to get back to your 60/40 target allocation. But at any time, if you're in the middle of a bull run, you're selling off some of the assets that have performed well recently and buying the ones that haven't!

Yet, since no one knows exactly what the market will do in the short term, it's the best way to make sure that you keep the allocation that works for you in both bull and bear markets. Rebalancing once or twice a year is a good practice to have.

If you haven't rebalanced in a while, this is a good exercise along with revisiting your goals. You may find that you need to change your allocation in order to meet your revised targets.

- Keep adding money consistently

In order to build a solid nest egg, the best way to invest is to have an automatic deduction from your paycheck or bank account that's transferred immediately to your investment account, whether it's a retirement account or not. Automatic transfers help take the emotion out so that no matter what the market's doing, you're investing. Your investment account should be set up so that the money is automatically invested when it hits the account as well, so you can't just let it sit in cash when there's fear in the market. You'll be buying on sale during bear markets, which is an excellent opportunity.

- Avoid hair-trigger reactions

The stock exchange is something that's developed only in the past 200 to 400 years (depending on how you characterize a market), and our human ancestors didn't have anything like this while they were fending off predators on the African savannah, or spreading across the globe afterward. Our brains are not optimized for numbers, rapid trading activity, blinking lights, and so on.

All that is to say that your gut feelings simply do not work when it comes to dealing with the stock market. Humans are very good at reading where another person is in the social hierarchy, which is a skill that our ancestors needed, and not at all about what a certain movement in a stock or stock market means. Therefore, any gut feelings you're having should probably be ignored in the context of trading.

As you learned earlier, humans have a bias against taking risks, and losses are very painful. So when you see a loss in your portfolio, you may very well feel some fear and worry, and you'll probably want to stop the pain—usually by selling out. Avoid acting on this impulse.

It works the same the other way too. When the market is going up and you think you've missed out on some easy action, the impulse is to buy the next thing that will ease the pain of missing out. Or your neighbor brags about how much money they made on 1800sockpuppets.com and you decide you need to get into the dot-com action and buy 1800sockpuppetsarestupid.com. Avoid acting on these impulses too. Neither one is going to end well.

- Don't lose perspective

In our culture, it is very easy to get caught up in what other people are doing (well, the Joneses just bought a $650,000 house and they only make $45,000 a year, so why shouldn't I?)

It's also very easy to get caught up in numbers because they're so simple to quantify. Yesterday 1800sockpuppetsarestupid.com was trading at $2.19 and now it's at $2.25 – we're in for the ride of a lifetime because the number went up, which is what it's supposed to do.

It's also not hard to forget where your portfolio started from. Maybe you had $1,000 originally and you've added an additional $1,000 over time. However, with the bull run, maybe your portfolio is up to $6,000. And then the bear comes, and it drops to $4,800. Yikes! Panic! But in fact, you only contributed $2,000 so you're actually still up $2,800.

And if you don't need any of this money for ten years, it doesn't really matter that much if it drops for a couple of years as long as you don't sell at the lower prices and lock in your loss. If you stay patient, you'll capture those upsides that can happen during and right after a bear market.

Look at your portfolio as a whole and what it's intended to do for you. It's your money, so it doesn't matter what the Joneses are doing. Daily fluctuations are typical in any kind of market, so if you're tracking your numbers too closely because it's easy to see whether a number is less or more than it was yesterday, you'll lose sight of the fact that you're investing for the longer term.

Given your risk tolerance, you know what kind of return you can expect from your money as an average over ten years. The fluctuations in between aren't really that meaningful, so don't try to derive some meaning from them.

- Take opportunities

Some types of stocks do better in downturns than others (you'll learn about them a bit later in the book.) Stocks that pay *dividends* to their investors can help you earn some income during the bear that you can invest.

You might also invest in some *actively managed* mutual funds that manage risk for you, by lowering their exposure to certain stocks or otherwise responding to market conditions. Passively managed funds, often index funds, don't offer these benefits but typically are less expensive in terms of management fees.

- Talk to a financial advisor

Having an objective third party to take a peek at your portfolio and discuss whether you need to take active measures may be helpful. Although humans tend to be action-oriented —when we're in pain we want to do something—very often the best course of action in a bear market is to do nothing unless you spot some strategic opportunities.

An advisor can help you walk through what might happen if you take a specific action compared to not taking it, or give you some ways to get perspective on what's going on. They may also have some recommendations as to how to adjust your portfolio when your goals or timeframes change and help you stay on track no matter how the market is performing.

HOW BEARS AFFECT YOUR BRAIN

Earlier you discovered the cognitive bias known as loss aversion. You now know that the human brain comes pre-wired with cognitive biases, and these have nothing to do with how intelligent you are. They're a result of how humans developed as a species in an environment where we had to survive other predators.

Back then there were no screens, stocks, houses, cars, or even chairs. Certainly, there was no such thing as bootstrapping your way up, and individualism could get you killed. There were animals that could eat us, and humans basically survived by living together in tribes and using our big brains to socialize with each other and find food together.

Now, of course, humans don't have any predators. However, human brains are finely tuned for being with other humans as part of a group and knowing where we are on the hierarchy of that group. The higher status you have, of course, the more resources you have access to. And anyone who was cast out of the group back then could very well die as a result, so humans have a fierce need to belong and some cognitive biases are a result of that.

There are a few biases that tend to crop up either at the end of a bull or during a bear which can lead to more pain and/or more losses during the market decline.

At the end of the bull, many investors are experiencing the consequences of these biases as well as overconfidence:

- FOMO

The fear of missing out is definitely a social-driven bias. When your group or your tribe is making money or at least bragging about it, you feel like you've got to make money too in order to avoid being cast out of the group. Of course, by that time investors have run prices up, even on stocks that don't have much long-term appeal, so you're making bad choices.

- Representativeness

Humans tend to draw conclusions from a small sample size and assume that's representative of the whole. Our ancestors had to get good at making quick decisions to avoid being eaten by tigers, and so they didn't want to stop and consider every single option when they believed there was a tiger in the area.

But although that's how human brains work, that's not how the modern world works. There are vanishingly few situations in which you have to worry about being eaten by a predator! (Unless you're a poacher, in which case, what goes around comes around.) You can't draw conclusions based on a few data points, but we have a tendency to do it.

People tend to believe that stocks will keep going up because they have been going up for the past day, month, week, or year. That's a relatively small sample. When you pull back and look at the history of the stock market, you see that at some point prices cease to rise.

- Familiarity

Humans like things that they've been exposed to and are familiar with. During a bull run, if there are specific stocks or sectors that have been doing well, that's what investors tend to pile into because it's familiar. The news has been talking about it, their friends and colleagues have been talking about it, and even if they don't know exactly how it works they're familiar with it.

Needless to say, once that stock or industry has reached the end of its run, there's a lot of pain waiting for the investors who didn't diversify into stocks and industries that are out of favor. You may have been told not to put all your eggs in one basket, but that's surprisingly difficult when that one basket is the only thing you're hearing about.

However, once the bear starts, these may come into play.

- Anchoring

This particular cognitive bias comes up a lot, not just in investing. Humans tend to *anchor* to the first piece of information that we've been given. If you read online that the average price of the car you're looking for is $30,000 and the first dealer you go to offers $29,900 you might snap it up because it's less than you were expecting.

However, maybe in your area, the car sells for $25,000 and other dealers offer $24,995. But you anchored to that first piece of information and stopped looking to see if there were better deals elsewhere.

In a bear market, you might anchor to the events that launched or at least coincided with the bear. Maybe it was a high inflation rate, and as long as the inflation rate remains high, you miss out on other positive economic news (such as a low unemployment rate, for instance).

You might decide that either the bear won't end fast enough or that the news is so bad there's no way you can stay invested. You end up selling when prices are low because you need to end the physical pain of watching your portfolio drop.

- Status quo bias

With this bias, you prefer to let things stay the same out of inertia or by staying with a previous decision when you would be better off making a change.

Suppose you sold out in the middle of a bear and have cash in your account. Even when signs point to the market getting better, you might stay in cash, which means losing out on those big positive days that often happen during a bear. You've already sold out and now it seems very hard to get back in the game, so you stick with the cash.

Being aware of cognitive bias can help, but you need some more concrete strategies to make sure you don't make bad decisions based on these hardwired errors in thinking.

AVOID ACTING ON YOUR EMOTIONS

Bear markets can be a significant test of your emotions. By putting guardrails in place, you can avoid making emotion-driven decisions that may make you feel better temporarily but that will cause serious damage to your nest egg.

There are three main ways emotions get you in trouble when it comes to investing.

1. They don't let you assess risk rationally

The human brain contains a lot of components, systems, and structures that have been adapted from other animal brains over time. You've probably heard of the *reptile* or *lizard brain*, which governs things like the fight-or-flight reaction when we feel like we're under threat. If there's a tiger ready to pounce and eat us, there's no time to stand around considering the pros and cons of running away or ignoring the tiger, or standing your ground. Fast, decisive action is required. The *mammalian* brain is linked to emotions, among other things.

The part of the brain that's responsible for making lists of pros and cons, sifting through numbers or spreadsheets, thinking about stocks as they relate to a nest egg, and other similar tasks is relatively new in human development and is also very slow and takes up a lot of energy.

So when your brain thinks it's under threat—and a financial loss often qualifies as a threat—your brain shuts down the slow, resource-draining *thinking* part and starts engaging the older systems instead.

Also, human emotional power is linked to how vivid something is. We react more strongly to stories that are salient and emotionally powerful. Humans are also notoriously bad at predicting how we'll feel in any given situation. It may be easy to decide how you'll act in a bear market, but you may feel much more anxious and fearful in the moment than you expect. Plus, the actions of others (especially the "tribe") heightens fear and anxiety.

2. They lead to short-term, quick decisions

Those strong negative feelings are likely to push you to want to take action. Who wants to be in a lot of pain? A bear market can be very painful, especially if you haven't experienced one before. You're hearing stories of people losing all their money, and that can make your own situation feel even worse.

So you really want to get rid of the pain, and the only way you think you can do that is to remove yourself from the market by selling out.

3. They prevent you from understanding probability

Frankly, humans aren't that great at understanding probability anyway. When it comes to investing, a bear market may seem like it will never end or that catastrophe is looming. The probability of an infinite bear market or total societal collapse is actually quite low.

But you'll hear lurid tales of negative occurrences which will feed your belief that this time, something is very wrong. You may hear stories about how much worse things can get, and whether or not they're likely to happen.

But don't worry, there are a number of ways that you can avoid letting your emotions get in the way. Later in the book, you'll discover specific strategies that will help take emotions out of investing.

- Stop paying so much attention to the market and your money

Long-term investors have no reason to look at their portfolio every day. If you pay too much attention, you'll start confusing the noise that is daily fluctuations in the market for signals and may end up making bad decisions.

Now that cable is 24/7, stations have to fill all that air time. Fear and greed are potent motivators, so you'll probably hear a lot of that being stoked. They used to say for local news that "if it bleeds it leads", and that's true of financial channels as well.

Don't confuse confidence for competence. No one knows what happens in the short-term, so even though the pundit predicting collapse sounds very confident about what he's saying, he doesn't know either. And he may very well have a financial reason for saying what he's saying (he's being paid.)

You're not going to learn anything from the financial news that should cause you to make a change in your portfolio. No one on the channel knows anything about you or your situation, so they can't make a good recommendation for you. And if there's no action for you to take, why bother listening to it? Have fun with your family and friends instead.

- Don't permit yourself to take action in the moment

If you're frantically typing in your investment account online so you can make a change, you're being driven by fear (or greed). You haven't made a rational assessment of the situation, and you've probably lost all perspective.

Instead, decide that you'll allow some period of time to elapse between when you hear a piece of news and when you act on it. Give yourself at least an hour, and potentially all night to sleep on it. If you're hearing about it on the financial news channel, everyone else has already heard it and the news is priced in. So you won't lose out on any special deals or bargains by allowing yourself time to think about it instead of feeling about it.

- Avoid bad timing

How do you make money with trading? Sell when prices are high and buy when they're low. However, for a variety of reasons, this can be hard to do! When everyone else is buying and you're suffering from FOMO, prices are already high. If the financial news is talking up a stock or industry, prices are already high. So if you're buying in at these times, you're buying high.

When the bull run is over and the bear market starts, everyone panics. No one wants to be last off the playground, and so people are selling in a frenzy. When prices are already low. And if the news has lots of stories on the market meltdown, then prices are already low. When you sell at these times, you're selling low.

Both of these are the exact opposite of what you should be doing. However, just because you made a mistake doesn't mean you have to make more mistakes. Suppose you succumbed to FOMO and bought while prices were already high. That doesn't mean when the selling starts that you have to do the same. You could just sit tight on your investments.

Eventually, when markets rise again, you could end up sitting on a nice profit.

- Studies show investors make bad decisions

Think you wouldn't make the mistake of bad timing? Unless you have proof from your behavior in a previous bear market, you probably would have before you read this book. Net mutual fund outflows (from investors selling out of their funds) peaked at just about the same time the market hit bottom in the Great Recession.[10] In other words, they sold low.

The best way to avoid bad market timing is to avoid trying to time the market in the first place, which you'll learn more about later in the book.

- Measuring fear and greed

There are a couple of indices that you can look at to determine whether there's a lot of fear and greed operating in the market. Why is that important? When you know the crowd is running on emotion, that is the exact time you need to stay calm, cool, and collected. Whether it's fear or it's greed, investing based on emotion leads to bad decisions.

One such index is the VIX, which measures the volatility (price fluctuations) in the S&P 500 index. When the VIX is relatively quiet, there's not much "vol" in trading, which means it's not particularly emotional. But when the VIX is moving, emotions are running high.

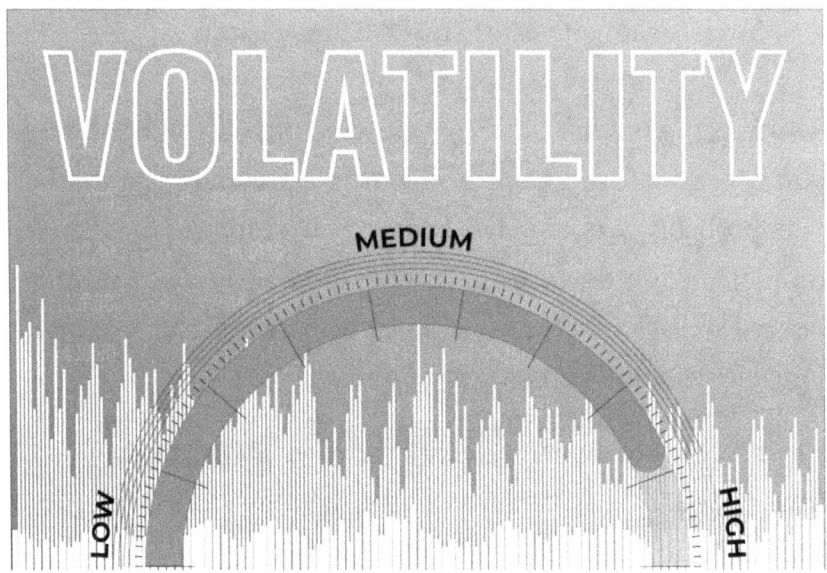

This index actually tracks the price of options on stocks, such as puts and calls. We'll talk later in the book more about what these options mean, but basically, when the VIX is high, the options are more expensive because they're in high demand.

When it's low, the cost of options is less expensive because investors aren't trying to hedge their bets. A level of 20 or higher is considered high, whereas less than 20 it's low and the market is less volatile.

CNN Money publishes the Fear and Greed Index, which scores the market on seven different indicators from 0 to

100. If the total score on all the factors averages up to 50 or more, the market is operating on emotion.

The seven indicators are as follows.[11]

1. Price momentum

This gauges how far off the market's moving average it is. Close to the average means less volatility and emotion.

2. Price strength

How many stocks are hitting trailing 52-week highs vs. trailing lows. In other words, if most stocks are hitting highs, emotions may be in charge.

3. Price breadth

This measures trading volumes in rising stocks compared to trading volumes in declining stocks, which can help you determine whether greed or fear is leading.

4. Options

Call options are generally indicative of positive sentiment because it gives you the option to buy the stock once the price reaches a certain target. Put options are generally negative because they allow you to sell stocks once the target is reached. If call options are running ahead of puts, there's a greed signal; if puts are in greater demand then there's a fear signal.

5. Junk bond attractiveness

High-yield bonds, formerly known as junk bonds, are more popular when investors want to take on more risk (typically a greed signal.) Measuring the spread between junk bond yields and investment grade bonds shows whether greed has taken over.

6. Volatility

This index includes the VIX, as explained above.

7. Safety attractiveness

US Treasuries are considered essentially risk-free. The difference in demand between stocks and Treasuries can indicate emotion as well.

- Key trading strategy to manage emotions

The best way to manage through bear markets (and bulls as well) is to have an investment plan. Know what you're buying, when you're buying it, and why. You can add some rules into it (such as "I will wait 24 hours to take action on a piece of news, whether good or bad.")

Not having a plan puts you at the whims of your emotions, and you now know how much damage emotions can do to your portfolio.

AVOID ACTING ON THE "WISDOM" OF THE CROWD

Crowds are comprised of a number of individuals who have their own reasons for investing (or selling), their own reasons for optimism or pessimism regarding the market, and different ways in which emotions can drive their decisions. The masses drive the market, but they're often wrong.

The crowd has its own herding nature, which can influence otherwise logical individuals to go along with the masses. Interestingly, the fear of missing out on profits is more intense than the fear of losing your life savings.[12] Our need as social beings can strongly influence investors to go along with the crowd.

It also serves as a type of leader, especially if you don't have a plan or you're doubtful about your own capabilities. If everyone else is doing it, there must be some reason, right? It can't just be the madness of crowds. (Actually, very often it is, but that's not how most people think about it.)

You do have a choice as to whether or not you decide to follow the crowd. Sometimes it's in your best interests to do so. When's that? When your own independent analysis based on your investing plan coincides with that of the crowd. But if your analysis shows something different from what the masses are doing, cut and run.

It does take conviction to go against the crowd, but just because everyone else is taking a certain course of action, that doesn't mean it's the right thing to do. (Remember that everyone took their money out of mutual funds at the bottom of the market. Bad decision, but that's what the masses did.)

Your investment plan will help guide you on whether to follow or take your own path. Understanding what you're buying (and selling) and why will give you a basis for making decisions that are logical and not based on emotions—whether they're the masses or your own.

Unfortunately, the market is under no one's control. You can do all the due diligence that you can (and should), but that doesn't mean the market can't deliver a surprise or two. And mass psychology plays a part as well. When greed is on the rise, bubbles tend to form. And when fear's on top, not only do bubbles pop, but valuable stocks can lose value in the marketplace and appear to be bad trades.

Having a plan is a good way to avoid the madness. Some investors even adopt a contrarian stance, where they buy when fear is running rampant and sell when a bull market is on a tear. However, that may require leaning a bit more on market timing, which is often a bad idea. Plus, crowds aren't always wrong.

The madness of crowds goes back hundreds of years, probably even past "tulip mania" in the Netherlands in the 1600s. It's nothing new, but the fast pace of the modern world could mean you'll get wiped out much more quickly.

CHAPTER SUMMARY

One big factor in outlasting a bear market and making a profit from it is to avoid giving in to emotions and cognitive biases that don't help investors. Bear markets don't last forever, so it's a matter of being able to handle your emotions and prevent being caught up in the madness of the crowd. One of the most effective ways to make sure your investment strategy is based on logic and your personal situation is to have a plan and understand why you're making the investment decisions. By playing along with all the bear markets that come along, you'll be able to profit from them and make money no matter what the market is doing.

The next secret is about avoiding market timing.

3

WHAT TIME IS BETTER FOR INVESTING?

In earlier chapters, we've mentioned market timing. You may be wondering why it's so important to avoid. Here you'll discover that trying to time the market is an impossible game, and what's really important if you want to make money is time *in* the market.

What is market timing, anyway?

The term market timing refers to moving money in and out of various investments according to a method that's supposed to be predictive. After all, everyone knows that you make money when you get in at a low price point and then sell at a high one. So if you can get in at the right time and then out at the right time, you'll make lots of money.

That's the theory behind it, anyway. In practice, timing the market is pretty much impossible over the long term, though occasionally traders find success briefly. Some day traders, professional money managers, and portfolio analysts use charts and other types of analyses to time the market. But in general, over time they do no better than buy-and-hold investors.13

As you might guess from the name, a buy-and-hold strategy is one where you purchase investments and hold onto them and allow them to appreciate, rather than trying to figure out exactly when is the best time to buy in and when the best time to sell is.

These trades are usually focused more on the investor's investment strategy and result from a plan to achieve financial goals. Having said that, even buy-and-hold investors don't want to buy in at too high a price or sell when the investment is at a low.

Buy-and-hold doesn't require much effort on the part of the investor, but trying to time the market requires good knowledge of the markets and a lot of time and energy spent on analysis. There are some advantages to timing, as well as disadvantages.

- Advantages
- Good for short-term goals

Market timing is a strategy that only works for short periods of time. Even professional investors can't get it consistently right over a longer time horizon. But if you're looking at a goal that's approaching quickly, this technique might work.

- Avoid volatility

When you're a buy-and-hold investor, you'll be riding out recessions and downturns to capture the upside after the market turns. Which means you're in for a rough ride. But if you can time entering and exiting the trade, you'll enjoy a smoother ride. Once you're out of the trade, things will probably be more volatile since you're selling before the investment begins to lose money.

- Bigger profits

Assuming you can time your buys and sells exactly right (which is a very big assumption!) you'll be buying in at a very low point, if not the actual bottom, and selling at a high, if not the absolute top.

When you don't time your trades, you may be getting in when it's relatively low and out when it's relatively high. However, you probably won't capture as much of the growth as you would by timing perfectly.

- Losses reduced

You won't be subject to the losses that come with a price decline because you'll be out of the trade before that happens. Instead of riding out the pain (and potentially succumbing to it by selling out when you shouldn't), you won't be experiencing it in the first place.

- Disadvantages
- Timing is hard

Trading volume just on the New York Stock Exchange is in the billions each day.[14] Not only are you competing with other human traders, but some of them are computers that trade algorithmically and much faster than any human. Not to mention that many of these traders are experts and trading is what they do all day.

Most professional timers use computer-generated charts and other types of statistical analysis and models that you probably don't have access to. Your spreadsheet is unlikely to compete with what a pro works with every day. They're also familiar with how the market works and have experience with how emotions affect decisions.

And even with all this armor, they still don't have much of an advantage over someone who just buys and holds their investments.

- Costs are higher

In order to trade, you have to pay fees. These expenses may be reduced for high-volume traders, like the computer algorithms and professional portfolio managers, but you probably aren't going to qualify for a bulk discount.

If you're doing a lot of trades, then you're going to be paying a lot more fees compared to someone who's in it for the long term.

- More attention to the markets is necessary

In the last chapter, you learned that a great way to avoid investing with your emotions is to ignore the markets and stop checking up on your portfolio so frequently. But if you want to time the market, you pretty much have to make the market your day job. Opportunities can appear and then vanish in a matter of minutes, so you're always on the lookout when you're market timing.

- Tax disadvantaged

Quick note on taxes: the IRS requires you to pay *income tax* on the income that you make (your W-2 if you work for someone else, or your 1099 if you're a freelancer or contractor) as well as *capital gains tax* on assets that you sell.

The capital gains tax is on the difference between your *basis*, or what you paid for the asset, and its sale price. You may owe capital gains tax when you sell your house or other real estate, and when you sell investments (as long as they're not in tax-advantaged retirement accounts.)

If you bought stock in 1800sockpuppetsarestupid.com at $2.50 per share and sold it at $3.50, you would pay tax on $1.00 per share, which is the capital gain, on the sale. However, there are two types of capital gains taxes: short-term and long-term.

As long as you wait a full year between buying and selling the asset, you get long-term treatment on the gains. That means your tax could be anywhere from 0% to 15%, though some high-earning taxpayers might have to pay 20%.[15]

On your $1.00 per share, if your income is low enough you might pocket the entire dollar, or you pay 15% and retain $0.85 profit.

However, if you hold the asset for less than a year, as market timers typically do, you get short-term treatment. The short-term capital gains tax is your marginal income tax rate. So if you're in the 24% tax bracket, you'll pay 24% on the gains.

In that case, you'd pay $0.24 tax on your $1.00 gain and keep $0.76. If you're in a higher tax bracket than 24%, you'd pay higher taxes for your short-term gain.

FAILURES OF MARKET TIMING

The millions of investors who trade on the stock exchange have different timeframes and different reasons for buying and selling. That makes reading charts and doing analysis more difficult, because the signals get muddled amid all the varying viewpoints. If the market is clearly heading for a downturn or clearly heading for an upturn it's already too late to try to time it.

But you don't have to take my word for it - we've got research done by Charles Schwab in 2021, simulating five different styles of investing. It assumes that each investor received the same amount of cash at the beginning of each year for twenty years and then compared the compounded returns. Each investing style had the same portfolio allocation, so the only difference in the returns came from when each investor put their money in.

The five styles were as follows:

   1. Perfect market timing

The study assumed that this investor put all the money in at the lowest bottom of the year. (Naturally, this would actually be really hard to do in real life.)

   2. Lump sum ASAP

This investor dumped the entire amount into the market, according to the specified allocation, on the first trading day of the year. (You probably will not have all your money for the year available on January 2.)

3. Dollar-cost averaging (DCA)

You'll discover more about this technique later in the book because it can be incredibly helpful during bear markets. For this investor, the amount of cash was divided into twelve equal installments and invested on a specific date each month.

4. Peak Investor

This investor was unlucky enough to put all the money in at the peak trading day of the year. (Fortunately, this would also be difficult to do in real life.)

5. Never invested

Here the investor kept waiting for a good time to get in the market – but never did, leaving all the money in cash instead. (Unfortunately, this is an all-too-easy trap to fall into in real life.)

The results might surprise you. As you might expect, the perfect market timer had the most money at the end of the twenty years. However, the lump sum ASAP was a close runner-up, as was the dollar-cost average. Second and third place were within 11% of the perfect market timer—and spent a lot less time and energy on their investing.[16] Interestingly, even the peak investing strategy worked better than not investing at all. (which we'll get into in the next section.)

However, you will still hear investors talk about market timing. While the leading German stock picker Uwe Lang believes that buy-and-hold is not a good strategy, he spends his entire day working in the markets, as others who promote market timing typically do.[17] You might even hear supporters of timing mention a winning edge, but be wary of anyone who's trying to sell you something!

If you're still interested in timing but know that you won't be able to do it perfectly, one way to strike the balance between these opposing viewpoints is to invest in a *tracker fund*, which will fluctuate up and down with the market.

But if you decide that market timing isn't worth it, you should still pay attention to your investing and trading. Make sure you have the right allocation so you're taking the right amount of risk, and rebalance periodically as you learned to do earlier in the book.

TIME *IN*, NOT TIM-*ING*

Now that you understand how difficult it is to time the market and how much time and energy you need to try to do it, you know that a buy-and-hold strategy is much easier and gets you almost the same results. But the key to the buy-and-hold strategy is that you have to buy investments, and you have to hold them.

If you're dollar-cost-averaging your investments, then the "buy" part of the equation isn't so hard. It's the "hold" portion that most investors have difficulty with. When your portfolio starts dropping, it can be hard for many people to stay invested. We've discussed some techniques to help you take the emotion out of investing.

Another fact that might help is that the longer you stay in the stock market, the more positive your outcome – even though you'll have plenty of highs and lows as you stay in. The Capital Group (American Funds) looked at 91 years of stock market history and found that over a year-long period, there are 66 positive years (and 25 negative ones.)

But looking at three-year timeframes within those 91 years, the positive periods increase to 74, with only 15 negative three-year periods. Over five-year lookbacks, there are 76 positive periods, and if you look at timeframes of a decade or more, there are 77 positive periods, which means 94% of the time the outcome was positive.[18] This shows that the longer you can hang on, the more likely you'll be happy with the result and build your nest egg.

Your investments will be worth much more when you stay invested and capture all the best-performing market cycles. According to a study by Merrill Lynch, if you invested $1,000 at the beginning of 1991 and held it until the end of the year 2020, you'd have a little over $21,000.

If you tried to time the market and did it wrong, missing out on the 10 best months, you'd only have a little over $8,000—less than half the amount, just from not being invested in the best ten of about 360 months. Miss the top twenty months and you would have almost $4,000 or less than one-fifth of the total.[19]

As you can see, whatever you need to do to stay invested through the tough times will be worth your while!

WHAT GOES WRONG WHEN YOU WAIT TOO LONG

On the other hand, maybe the "hold" part of the equation isn't the problem. For some reason, you've decided not to put in a certain amount of money every month, or maybe you have a lump sum waiting to be invested. But you're having a hard time deciding when is a good time to invest. Months go by and your money is still sitting in a checking or savings account.

As you saw earlier in the chapter, even bad market timing where you get in when prices are high every time is still better for your portfolio in the long run than letting everything sit in cash. You may recall the Charles Schwab study with the five investing styles, where perfect market timing, investing at the beginning of every year, and dollar-cost averaging came in pretty close to one another.

Let's take a closer look at the numbers. In each scenario, the amount to be invested each year was $2,000 every year from 2001 to 2020. Note that this investing period includes the Great Recession of 2008-2009!

Perfect market timing, which even proponents of market timing would agree is pretty much impossible over the short term, resulted in a balance of nearly $151,400. The first "runner-up" was lump sum ASAP, investing the money on the first trading day of the year, with about $135,400. Next was dollar-cost averaging at roughly $134,800. (Although, you could consider the lump sum ASAP a type of dollar-cost averaging since a specific amount was invested each year on a specific date.)

Farther behind was the peak investor, who perfectly market timed in the wrong way by putting money in at the peak of the year. They still ended up with roughly $121,100. Not as good as the other three, but that's still a significantly positive number.

Now you may be asking, OK, but what happened to the one who never invested and left everything in cash? A little over $44,400. Not even half what the investor who invested at exactly the wrong time every year made.[20]

In all fairness, it's psychologically very difficult to invest a sum of money and watch it drop the very next day, which is what would have happened to the bad timer. But as long as the bad-timer held onto their investments and didn't sell out, they still would have done very well over that time period.

That means you could get it wrong every time – investing near the top – and still be better off over the long run than if you kept waiting for the "right" time to invest. It's highly unlikely you'd get it wrong every time, particularly if you dollar-cost average. Pick an amount and a date and automate it (we'll get into that in the next chapter.)

There's an old Chinese proverb that says the best time to plant a tree was twenty years ago. The second-best time is now. Investing is the same way – the best time to put your money to work was twenty years ago. The next best time is today.

CHAPTER SUMMARY

While you know you're supposed to buy low and sell high, in the real world it's very hard to get the entrances and exits exactly right. Market timing requires a lot of time and attention to the market and your portfolio. Interestingly, you'll get almost the same results simply by investing regularly and staying invested in what's known as a buy-and-hold strategy. That's because time in the market is more important than timing your buys and sells. Avoiding market timing helps you make money in a bear market so that you've got good performance no matter whether the market is up or down.

In the next chapter, you'll discover more about dollar-cost averaging.

4

DOLLAR-COST AVERAGING IS YOUR ALLY

In the last chapter you learned that dollar-cost averaging, or DCA, can actually perform pretty well when done consistently. It has the additional benefit of helping take emotions out of your investing, which as you know is especially important when the market is dropping.

WHAT IS DCA AND WHEN IS THE BEST TIME TO USE IT?

At this point, you likely understand the fundamentals: investing regularly with a certain amount of money that you've determined beforehand. You split the total into roughly equal amounts to invest at each point.

It's important to recognize that dollar-cost averaging is not just putting cash aside at regular intervals. You don't earn anything on cash. When you're using DCA, you're actually investing your cash into something that will generate some compounding returns for you. It's also not a strategy that works very well with short-term investments, because a lump sum usually works better when your goal is less than a few years away.

If you participate in a 401(k) or similar retirement plan at work, you're probably dollar-cost averaging these investments. You've told them what percentage of your salary to set aside for investing before the check even hits your bank account. Whatever that amount is gets invested every paycheck, typically monthly or biweekly.

Because it happens automatically, you may not pay too much attention to the price of the investments every time you make a purchase. That takes the emotion out of your investing, as long as you don't panic and stop buying stocks altogether when the market stops dropping. What may not be as obvious is how powerful this technique can be in a bear market, when you're buying on sale.

Let's check out an example of how this looks in the real world in a variety of scenarios. Suppose you're interested in a tech company named Jekyll with a ticker symbol of JKL and you're planning to invest $1,000. The price is usually around $50 per share.

You've identified three different price targets to sell the stock: $40 so you can curb your losses; $60 to take some profit off the table; and $80 to get off the rollercoaster before it starts speeding downward. Here's how the various scenarios play out.

- Lump sum at $50

If you buy the stock at $50, you'll end up with 20 shares. Ignoring taxes and fees, you sell at $40 per share which is $800 total. Since you invested $1,000, you have a loss of $200. If you sell at $60 per share or $1,200, you have a $200 profit. And at a price point of $80 per share or $1,600, you net $600.

- DCA in a bear market

This technique really shines in a declining market, because you're scooping up bargains as the price decreases. Suppose you're investing $1,000 every quarter, so you have $250 to invest four times a year.

In a bear market, suppose that you buy at $50, $45, $40 (which marks the 20% bear decline), and $35. At the first price point ($50) you end up with 5 shares ($250/$50); at the second with 5.56; the third with 6.25, and the fourth with 7.14 shares. In total, you now have 23.95 shares.

Now when it comes time to sell, your loss of $40 won't be so severe, and you'll have even bigger gains at the higher prices. If you sell your 23.95 shares at $40, you net $957.54, so your loss is only $42.06. Compare that to the lump sum loss of $200!

Your net gain at $60 is $436.90 (compared to $200 with the lump sum) and at $80 your profit is $915.87 (vs. $600). As you can see, buying on sale when the market is down really pumps up your profits.

- DCA in a market that's not moving much

Some markets move sideways rather than up or down for a period of time. Eventually, you'll see a bull or a bear start running, but for a short period, you really don't see a trend. Suppose your $250 is used to buy at the following price points: $50, $45, $52, $47. You'll end up with 20.68 shares of JKL, not far off from the 20 lump-sum shares.

At a sale price of $40, you'll net a loss of $172.70. At $60 your net gain is $240.94, and at $80 it's $654.59. You do a bit better than the lump sum, but it does depend on whether you can pick up some bargains when the market is sideways or not.

- DCA in a rising market

This will not look like the best choice. Suppose your buys are at $50, $55, $60, and $65. In this case, you'll only have 17.59 shares. If you sell them at $40 your net loss is $297.67, and at

$60 you barely have a profit ($53.50). At $80 your net profit comes to $404.66.

Now you might be wondering, does dollar-cost averaging really work? After all, in a rising market, the numbers don't look great. However, bear (!) in mind that no one knows what's going to happen next in the market. Maybe it's rising, but maybe it's not. Do you want to roll the dice on making a lump sum and then having the market decline or go sideways, where DCA may be a better choice?

Another caveat is that you're looking over the long term. The examples above are relatively short-term, but as the holding period grows, the differences may not be as significant. There are three main benefits to dollar-cost averaging:

1. Take emotion out of investing

Basically, dollar-cost averaging helps you get out of your own way. As we discussed in the last chapter, many people find it hard to get started because they can't find a good entrance point.

By deciding that you'll invest $100 on the 10th of every month (for example) and automating that decision so the money's automatically taken out of your bank account, you don't have to look at the stock market at all. Nor do you need to frequently look at your portfolio. The money's going into the investment account and automatically buying into the investment(s) you've chosen. It doesn't matter if the market's going up, down, sideways, or in circles… you're investing. You'll be able to capture dips along the way, but you won't have to be worried about the market dipping because you don't have to pay attention to it.

You'll stay off the FOMO rollercoaster and avoid buying in when prices are high, or buying an investment that doesn't really make sense because "everyone else is doing it". You've already made your decision, and you've implemented it.

2. Avoid timing the market wrong

You might think prices are low and it's a good time to get in… but then the market goes lower and you're worried about investing when the market has gone haywire. Or prices are already high and you think they have room to run, but in fact, you've hit the peak and it's downhill for months on end from there.

By dollar-cost averaging, you're removing these kinds of decisions from your process. It's very easy to misread market signals or start believing the hype. But when you're just investing a certain amount periodically (and you don't have to lift a finger to make it happen), you've made the choice and don't have to worry about whether now's a good time or not.

3. Think long-term

Your financial goals like retirement are likely long-term, and thinking long-term helps you align your money process with those goals. Over the long-term, stocks tend to rise 8-10%. But you don't see that in daily trading.

When you're thinking in terms of decades, not days or even months, you can see what's important about investing (staying invested in the market). It's easier to put aside more trivial matters, like whether your portfolio is up a dollar since yesterday or not.

It's also easier to have a good perspective on declining markets, knowing that in the long term this too shall pass. They may be painful or seem interminable in the short term, but bears put away their claws and lumber away at some point. When you have a shorter-term perspective, you're worried about things that aren't so relevant to your investing goals and may cause you to make bad decisions as a result.

DOLLAR-COST AVERAGING IN A BEAR MARKET

DCA helps you hedge your risk. If the market goes higher, the investments that you made earlier on appreciate more in price, especially as time goes on. At the same time, when you end up in a bear market, you're buying on sale.

You may even consider accelerating some of your investing when markets are dropping so that you're putting more money to work at lower price points. Now, this might sound a bit like market timing! But you can use dollar-cost averaging as your general strategy, and then opportunistically grab some bargains while you can.

You hear a lot about buying the dips, but the dips get deeper which means you get to buy at a significant discount. Since you can't time the markets exactly, investing regularly makes a lot of sense. You can look for companies that have strong fundamentals such as cash flow, and solid profits, and that are investing in growth.

As an example, maybe you have a windfall, inheritance, or another sum of money that you've decided to put to work over a six-month period. If the market starts heading downhill in, say, the third month, you might increase your usual amount to take advantage of the lower prices. You could consider investing the remainder, or you might invest a bigger portion and then wait for the next month to see if prices go even lower and again invest a bigger chunk.

It's highly unlikely that you'll be able to invest exactly at the bottom. If you were in the market during the Great Recession of 2008-2009, did you commit your capital on March 9 of 2009?[21] That was the absolute bottom – *but no one knew it at the time*. The absolute bottom is known only after the event.

If you'd been dollar-cost averaging during 2008-2009 you would have captured amazing bargains, but hardly anyone was doing that because the environment was really scary. Not all bears are so terrifying, but it's critical to understand that what seems easy when the markets are up suddenly becomes agonizing when prices start dropping.

DCA helps you stay invested while the bear is running. Not having to pay close attention to the markets can really help you when prices begin to decline! You know you have a system that's working on your behalf, and you're able to take the long view and allow the bear to run its course without panicking. Maybe you bought some investments at a high, but you also captured some lows.

You'll buy on sale, but also, you won't have to regret your investments (which may cause you to sell out to stop the pain). Imagine that you invested your $1,000 lump sum one day, and the very next day it's $800. You might start thinking that you invested in the wrong asset - and sell while the price is low, thus locking in your loss.

Or you might be afflicted with the "I shoulds": I should have waited to invest, I should have invested in something else, I should have split up my investments, I should have avoided putting all my money in one basket, etc.

You may recall from the last chapter that even investing perfectly wrong still gives you a better outcome than sitting in cash. But it's hard to avoid regrets, and one way to stop the pain of all these ruminations is to simply sell out.

If this sounds ridiculous to you, it isn't. People who aren't able to sit through a bear or through investing mistakes they've made can make even worse ones.

I personally know a woman who felt bad about an investment she'd made in her Roth IRA – the kind of IRA where you get to take the money out tax-free starting at age 59 ½ (as long as you follow the rules). She thought she had paid too much for the wrong investment.

She insisted on selling the investment and taking the money out completely. Even though it restarted the 5-year clock on a Roth IRA and caused her to lose money that she couldn't deduct from her taxes because it was inside a retirement account. All because she felt regret over an investment and wanted to get rid of everything that reminded her of the mistake.

I tried to reason with her but to no avail. She'd made a minor error that probably wouldn't have made a significant difference in the long run, but unfortunately, her emotions led her to make a huge one.

If she had used the DCA technique, she might not have had those regrets and would have avoided a significant decline in her investments. She might even have been able to pick up some bargains. And had she eventually decided that she did want to change the stocks she was investing in, she could have simply made the change in her investing program.

When you're investing for the long term, especially when you encounter a bear, you do need to give the investment time to perform. That's not measured in weeks or even months, but in years. We'll discuss some stocks that tend to perform better when the overall market is in decline later in the book. But if most stocks are doing badly and yours is too, that doesn't mean you chose poorly! Give it time to recover.

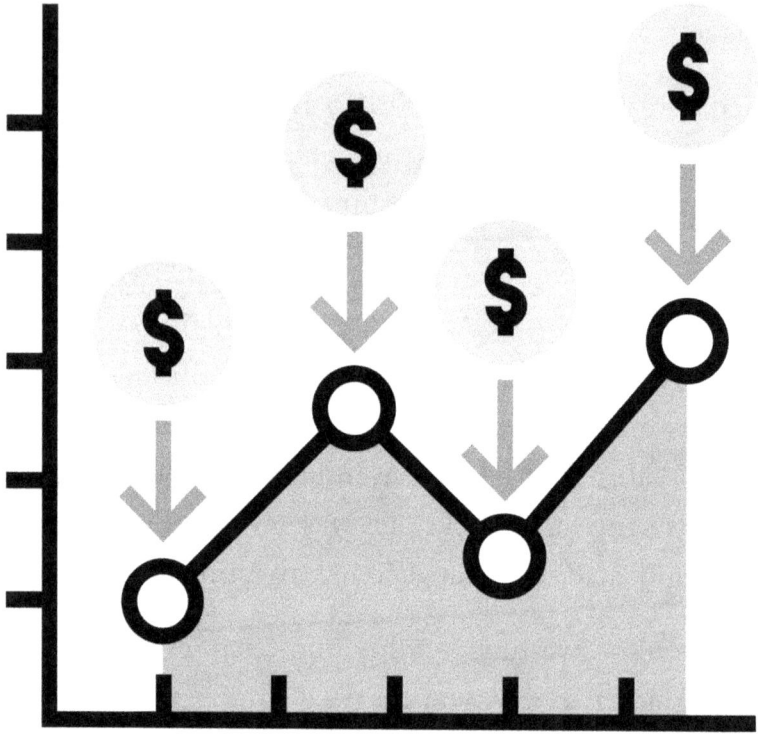

Buying low and selling high is the ultimate way to make money, and when you're in a bear market you've got plenty of opportunities for the first half of the adage: buying low. (You'll need to wait for a bull for the second half!) Load up on bargains when you can, and use dollar-cost averaging to help you take some of the fear out of buying when the market's declining.

Looking for some concrete examples of what to do with your DCA dollars in a bear market? There are a few ways to get smart about what you're buying.

- Diversify

We'll discuss this in more detail in the next chapter, but this is the stock market's way of saying "Don't put all your eggs in one basket". It doesn't just refer to buying more than one stock, but to buying more than one type of stock. For example, during the dot-com bubble, investors loaded up on dot-com stocks. Guess what happened when the bubble burst.

There are some sectors and industries that tend to weather declining markets pretty well, but again you don't want to buy into only one sector or industry with your money.

A broad-based index fund or ETF (exchange-traded fund), such as something that's based on the S&P 500, NASDAQ 1000, or MSCI-EAFE (international stocks), will give you exposure to a variety of companies in different industries and sectors.

- Strong businesses

If you prefer to buy stocks rather than funds or ETFs look for quality companies that will weather the downturn. You don't want to invest cheaply but still lose all your money because the bear takes down the company you invested in.

What makes a business more likely to survive? Look for companies that have name recognition and track records of stable and/or growing profits. A firm that has one spectacularly profitable year, but mostly doesn't make money, probably just got lucky that year and isn't a quality business.

You'll also want to highlight companies that have plenty of cash on hand. That allows them to ride out short-term disruptions and then be able to invest either back into operations or to return to shareholders.

A stock that pays dividends (and has a track record of doing so) is often a good choice. Again, some companies pay dividends once or twice and never again, so do your research if you plan to buy stocks. You can't rely on roundups or online article suggestions because you don't know how thoroughly the list was vetted.

- Look for low costs

You'll be more active than a lump sum investor when you invest every couple of weeks, month, or quarter. Make sure that the provider you're using for trades allows you to buy at low or no cost. Some platforms let you trade for free, but make sure you read the fine print and understand what the rules are.

This includes online trading platforms and apps. Some are known to suspend trading at their own whims, so their supposedly low-cost platform can come with a huge price if you can't make the trades you want. You shouldn't be making any spontaneous sales anyway, but a trading halt means you can't buy a specific stock either. That could be a problem when you're trying to take advantage of a bear market.

When the market recovers, you can gloat about how many shares you bought on sale. You'll have bigger gains on your low-basis stock. (Recall from earlier that your basis is just how much you paid for the asset.)

If you've still got questions, you might consider discussing with a financial planner whether the DCA technique works for your particular situation.

SAMPLE DCA IN A STEEPLY DECLINING MARKET

This time you're investing in a huge conglomerate named Ellemen that makes a lot of "stuff" that average people enjoy with a ticker symbol of LMN. You've done your research and you feel pretty confident it will outlast the next bear. It's been trading around $100, but prices are coming down rapidly.

Since the stock's moving so much, you've decided to buy in once a week with the same amount of money instead of plopping in all your cash on the 10th of the month as you usually do. For the sake of simplicity, we'll ignore fees and taxes.

The first week you buy in at $100. In the second week, the price drops to $95, so now your average cost is $97.50. The price drops to $90 in the third week, pushing your average price down to $95. And finally, the last week of the month brings a price of $88, so your average price to buy LMN is $93.25.

And you hold. And you hold. And you hold until the bear runs its course. A month or two later you're sitting pretty when the price goes back to $100. Just by dollar-cost averaging into your position, you've profited by $6.75 (7.24%).

It's hard to know when the bottom occurs. In this example, the bottom was the last week of the month, but it could very well have been in some other week. The average price would have been the same. Since it's not possible to predict a bottom, increasing your DCA periods (from monthly to weekly, for instance) may help you capture more opportunities if the market's highly volatile and moving fast.

Obviously, you'll need a low-cost platform to make this kind of investing work best, because you don't want your profits eaten up by trading fees and commissions.

HOW YOU CAN START USING DOLLAR-COST AVERAGING TO YOUR ADVANTAGE

To make DCA perform for your portfolio, you'll first need a plan. Once you've made your decisions, then you can start executing them. Making a plan before the next bear market hits is your safest bet because then you won't have to worry about anxieties over a declining market leading to suboptimal choices.

When everything's going well, that's the time to make your plan and implement it. You'll be more rational and long-term in your thinking when the market's up. Know that things will feel more difficult once prices start heading downward, and make it easy to do the right thing for your money.

1. Choose your amount

How much can you realistically afford to invest? If you want to invest more, take a hard look at your current spending habits. Are there any memberships that you could cancel? Any services that you no longer use? If you go out to eat every night, how much could you save if you only ate out once a week? All the savings can go towards your investments.

2. Choose your fighter (investments)

Remember that DCA works for assets like stocks over the long run, so plan for companies that you'll want to hold onto for at least 7-10 years. No speculative investments (like cryptocurrencies) or high-flyers that you want to take a chance on. You want assets that you can buy and hold onto for a while without really thinking too much about them.

3. Choose your dates

When will you be making these investments? Many investors add to their retirement accounts with each paycheck, which could be monthly or every two weeks. If you're not tying your investments to your paycheck, then pick a date like the 10th or 22nd, or the third Wednesday.

As an example, maybe you're able to find $50 a month to invest. Hey, a little is better than none when it comes to investing. You decide to invest in the BFHD (Big Fat Hairy Deal) index that covers both US and international companies. Finally, you pick the 23rd of every month to pop your $50 into BFHD through your favorite trading platform.

Make sure you automate the plan because otherwise, you'll miss out on the benefits of DCA. If you're contributing to a retirement account at work, that's generally done for you. But if not, you'll need to not only send the transfers from your bank account to the trading platform every period but also to actually buy shares of the investment automatically when your money hits the platform.

In the example above, you would have to set up your checking account to automatically transfer the $50 on the 23rd of every month. Then, you'd set up your account at the trading site to automatically invest in BFHD when your money hits the account. (You might have to set a specific date, like the 25th, for the trade to happen.)

Looking at the status of 401(k) plans is a good way to gauge how effective DCA is at helping investors stay the course when it comes to bear markets. Most Americans with a 401(k) plan have their contributions automatically deducted from their paychecks and invested, while Americans without employer-sponsored plans such as IRAs may not be using dollar-cost averaging.

During the Great Recession, only a small percentage (not even 4%) of 401(k) participants stopped contributing at all, and a larger (but still relatively small) number of them changed their investment mix.[22] Dollar-cost averaging is a great way, especially for more risk-averse investors, to stick to their plans because it's less painful when the market drops.

Without having to pay attention to how bad the bear market gets, investors are able to focus on the long-term perspective and avoid seeing the losses in their portfolios as the stock market drops. Those that remind themselves that they're buying bargains may also feel less anxious when the financial news is bad.

CHAPTER SUMMARY

Putting a predetermined amount of money to work regularly, without worrying about the performance of the market for timing, is a good way for investors to take advantage of a bear market. As prices drop, they can buy on sale and experience significant gains when the market goes back up.

The "set-it-and-forget-it" nature of DCA also means investors are less exposed to any financial bad news, which allows them to keep perspective and avoid making a bad decision from emotion. By using DCA to buy when prices are low, you can have good returns even in a bear market.

In the next chapter, you'll discover smart ways to diversify your portfolio during a bear market.

5

DIVERSIFY WITHOUT DISENGAGING

Earlier in the book we briefly mentioned diversification as a tool to help during bear markets. The benefits of being diversified in general are well-documented, and there are additional benefits to being strategic about diversifying your portfolio during a steep market decline.

You know now that it's pretty much impossible to time the market, or make sure that you're entering a trade when the stock is at its lowest and exiting at its highest price. Another investing factor that's impossible to know ahead of time is which market sector will be the highest-performing in any given time period.

Will this be the year for small companies categorized as growth stocks? Or maybe it's international that's going to carry the winning banner for the next six months. Perhaps instead real estate takes the top spot. You don't know, and neither does anyone else.

Sure, there are trends for when small growth companies "tend" to outperform in the market cycle, but that doesn't mean it's guaranteed. Given where the economy was in its cycle in 2013, no one expected that medium and small companies would blast past the 40% return mark, nor that large companies were going to top 30%. But that's exactly what happened.

Since you don't know what's going to happen in any given time period of a year or less, it's prudent to have exposure to everything in your portfolio. That way you don't miss out on the top performer. The flip side of this is that you will always have a loser in your portfolio as well!

There are a variety of asset classes that you can choose from when you want to diversify. Equities are one option. In addition to the size of the company, you can look at whether earnings are plowed back into the company to keep them growing (growth style) or whether they're returned to the shareholders in the form of dividends.

Another avenue for diversification within equities is geographic location. Many investors, especially in the US, tend to have a "home bias" where they prefer American stocks. But you can also look internationally to developed countries (generally benchmarked to the MSCI EAFE index) and developing countries too. There, the risk is higher, but so is the reward.

You don't have to stop at equities, though. In terms of growth and income, many investors like REITs. The real estate investment trusts act like mutual funds for real estate, and you can invest in REITs that are residential and others that cover commercial spaces. These two areas of real estate can perform very differently in a bear market.

In addition to bonds, you might also consider commodities, which are typically materials like corn and gold. Alternative fuels and renewable energy have also brought new interest to items like cobalt and lithium, which are used in high-tech batteries.

Maybe this all sounds interesting, but you're still not sure if spreading your risk out into different market baskets is the way to go. The case study for diversification is Enron. It was an apparently widely profitable energy company, but some growth was coming from shady accounting practices, and eventually, it blew up. The price plummeted to zero. Many of its employees had company stock in their retirement accounts too, and some had only Enron. Not only did they lose their jobs, they also lost their entire retirement savings.

If you invest in a "market basket" of stocks, with a little bit of everything (such as you might find in a broad-based index fund or ETF), you'll be affected by a company that's in the index blowing up. But you won't lose your entire investment.

Enron is also a great example of why you need to diversify your retirement account away from company stock. In some cases, if you're a director or executive at a company, you're required to hold some stock so you have "skin in the game". But you don't need to leave your entire portfolio in company stock.

If you have company stock in your retirement account, you won't pay taxes on any gains if you sell some stock and replace it with different investments. Diversifying is prudent. And it can be especially valuable during bear markets.

THE NECESSITIES OF DIVERSIFICATION IN A DOWN MARKET

What should you buy during a declining market? We'll go into a variety of investing ideas in the rest of the chapter, but we're not encouraging you to buy one or two and call it a day. Picking stocks is a hard thing to do. Sure, Warren Buffet does it. But he doesn't even have a computer in his office. All he does is read.

Extremely interesting things like a company's 10-K filings, which is the comprehensive annual report, including audited financial statements that disclose the company's financial health. It can easily be 100 pages long. You can also read shorter versions that are filed quarterly (10-Q forms).

Either way, if you're going to pick stocks like Warren Buffett, then you have to put in the research and reading time like Warren Buffett. He also has a smart business partner, Charlie Munger, to bounce ideas off and discuss investments. Do you also have a knowledgeable, experienced investing partner that you can talk to on a regular basis?

Even large companies fall in price over time and flatline at lower valuations. Cisco was the biggest player in the S&P 500 in the late 1990s, and now its price is roughly half what it was then. The same goes for AT&T and Bank of America.[23] Strong quality companies are accepted onto the index and then are no longer worthy years later, or they stay on but in a much-diminished capacity.

Unlike certain Best Dressed lists, it's not possible to know ahead of time who's likely to be in or out several years from now. Owning the entire index or the entire market is a smarter play, and when you're buying the bear, you're getting those quality companies at bargain prices. You'll own the winners without having to predict who's going to win.

Having said that, there are some broad categories of stocks that you might consider buying for a bear. There are certain types of companies that tend to hold up in value better than others when the market is down, so it's a good idea to make sure that they're included in your diversified portfolio.

PLAY DEFENSIVE

Some companies will churn out reliable earnings and dividends no matter what the market is up to. These are known as *defensive* stocks, as opposed to defense stocks that are involved in the war machine. They're generally well-established firms that have solid cash flow. In other words, we're not talking about startups or companies that have just started to earn profits.

Defensive stocks are typically well-known, have a broad base of appeal, and usually, it would take a pretty severe catastrophe for them to go out of business. Not something cyclical like a bear market. For that reason, they're less risky than other stocks. The flip side to this kind of safety, of course, is that they won't outperform when the market starts coming back.

- Advantages

You get a stock market return that beats inflation with lower risk. (Warren Buffett often chooses defensive stocks for his portfolio.)

As a group, they tend to have better risk-adjusted performance over time. The *Sharpe ratio* is a way to measure a stock's average return per unit of risk, measured as volatility. A stock that fluctuates a lot in price will have a lower Sharpe ratio, whereas a reliable earner has a higher one. The higher the Sharpe ratio, the better, and defensive companies often have high Sharpe ratios.

- Disadvantages

Because they're less risky, they provide less return when compared with other stocks when the market bounces back. Unfortunately, this often means that investors sell out at some point when a bull market is running because they're not performing as well as other stocks are.

However, that's the worst time to sell out – because a bear is likely just around the corner, which is when the defensive stock shines.

There are certain sectors that generally contain more defensive companies. They're not particularly correlated with the business cycle, so the fact that the cycle is in a downward direction doesn't affect them as much.

Utilities are a good example of defensive stocks because people need power no matter what the stock market might be doing. Consumer staples, which are necessities that consumers need to buy all the time like food and hygiene products, also maintain strong demand even when the market's declining. Likewise for healthcare stocks, because people get sick all the time.

People always need shelter, so apartment real estate investment trusts or REITs are also defensive. REITs are like mutual funds for real estate. However, office or commercial REITs aren't defensive because as business slows due to market cycles, so does real estate for business.

If you're looking for more specific ideas, here are some to get you started with defensive companies. (Note that these were recommended by Nasdaq's Investor Place.)[25]

- Campbell Soup (CPB)

Though you might associate Campbell's with the iconic white and red soup cans, there's a lot more inside the company. It also owns Swanson frozen dinners, Pace, Pepperidge Farm, and Prego. No matter what's happening in the world, people need to eat, and a lot of Americans eat Campbell's products. It also produces significant dividends for its investors.

- Coca-Cola (KO)

Like Campbell Soup, "Coke" isn't just the red and white bottles of soda. The company has about 200 brands under its corporate umbrella, as well as global brand recognition and a steady stream of cash flow. All that cash enables it to offer significant dividends to its shareholders as well.

- Archer-Daniels-Midland (ADM)

You may not be as familiar with this company, but it's a huge agricultural processing business. It owns processing plants and crop procurement facilities and is a big player in the crop storage and transportation industry. You can't get more pure food-related than this, and they also benefit from high food inflation as seen in 2021-2022.

Its track record for dividends is excellent, with dividend hikes for a running 47 years straight.

- Kimberly Clark (KMB)

While the brand may now mostly be known for its Kleenex tissues and Huggies diapers, there are a wealth of brands in KMB's corporate portfolio. It also provides a strong dividend yield for its investors.

- Eli Lilly (LLY)

This pharmaceutical firm is also recognized around the world and its medicines mostly focus on Alzheimer's disease, diabetes, obesity, and cancer. Lilly's work on COVID-19 antibodies has also driven significant profits for the firm.

- Lockheed Martin (LMT)

A defense stock that's also defensive, Lockheed Martin has many contracts with the US military that don't depend on stock market cycles and valuations. Most of its contracts are long-term, and it provides a solid dividend for its shareholders too.

- Consolidated Edison (ED)

It's one of the largest investor-owned utilities and operates mostly in New York state. It's primarily an electric and gas utility, and it's pushing into clean energy and renewables as well. Like the other businesses on this list, it provides a tasty dividend for its shareholders.

GROW IN A BEAR

While defensive stocks hold up well in a bear market, you might not think of growth stocks as the place to be in a downturn. Especially if you remember the dot-com bubble and subsequent crash around the turn of the century! But you get to buy them on sale during a bear, and then watch them rocket back up in price when the market's on the upswing.

What exactly is a growth stock? It's a company whose earnings (profits) are generally expected to outperform the market as a whole. Their price-to-earnings (P/E) ratio is usually high because investors factor in the expected high growth and price it accordingly. You'll see lower P/E ratios for defensive stocks because they're not expected to grow fast.

These types of companies tend to be newer in business, and they don't often pay dividends. They prefer to invest their profits back into the company to help it grow, rather than returning that money to the shareholders in the form of dividends.

In contrast, value stocks are considered good choices because their price is lower than what investors think the intrinsic value is. They often pay dividends. They're often companies that are past their growth phase and may be in industries that aren't growing much either.

Market timers like momentum stocks, which generally explode with the market. But the momentum usually doesn't last more than a day or two, and they're mostly bought and sold by day traders, not long-term investors.

Those who want to invest for the long-term in growth stocks are looking for the capital gains they'll get on the appreciation of the stock when they sell it later on. They're not looking for a steady income from dividends, and are willing to keep investing even as the price goes higher. As long as the company continues to grow, a price that looks high today will appear low in the future as the stock appreciates in price.

You'll find growth stocks in many different industries, but they do have some things in common. Typically they have unique product lines and often have patents on new technologies. As they continue to innovate, they may be able to capture a larger and larger amount of market share.

For example, at one time Microsoft was considered a growth company because it had office software that was new. As more users adopted it, it crowded out its competitors (including Lotus 1-2-3, which was the leading software package at an earlier time).

A current example of a growth stock is Amazon, which, believe it or not, started as an online bookseller in the dot-com era. In 2021 it was the 4th largest company by market capitalization. (which is computed by share price times the number of shares it has for the public to trade.)[26] It has always traded at a high P/E.

In its earlier years, Amazon also demonstrated another common trait of growth stocks, which is low or negative earnings. As hard as it may be to believe now, there was a time (before it thoroughly conquered the online commerce space plus cloud computing) when Amazon was unprofitable. Because growth stocks may be in new industries, dealing with new technologies, and plowing money back into operations so they can keep growing, they don't always show a profit as early as their investors might hope.

What growth stocks might you consider investing in now? There's a variety to choose from, though many are in tech and you don't want to put all your money in one sector. Some growth stocks are small in size (*small caps*) but others, like AMZ (Amazon) and Alphabet (GOOG) are large caps.

- Alphabet (GOOG)

Formerly known as Google, it started as a search engine during the dot-com era and has ballooned to a digital ad company. Before Google, you had to do a Boolean search online where "pink unicorn" would give you different results from "unicorn pink" which was also a different search from "pink and unicorn" which again was different from "pink or unicorn".

- Amazon (AMZ)

For literally all your online shopping and cloud computing leads.

- Block (SQ)

Formerly known as Square, this is a more recent entry into technology. It handles digital payments.

- Etsy (ETSY)

This eCommerce alternative started as more of a marketplace for small artisan businesses, but it's grown beyond that as well.

- MercadoLibre (MELI)

You might not be as familiar with MercadoLibre, but it's a huge digital payments company in Latin America.

- Meta (FB)

Formerly known as Facebook, the company is branching into its version of the "metaverse".

- Netflix (NLFX)

Another company that's been around a while, Netflix used to snail mail DVDs to its customers before streaming was invented.

- Salesforce (CRM)

If you're in business you might recognize this name as one of the premier client relationship management (CRM) applications out there, though its software has expanded well beyond CRM to other cloud business operations.

- Shopify (SHOP)

Another eCommerce company, Shopify helps businesses sell their wares online.

- Tesla (TSLA)

While it began as an electric car company that profited mostly from renewable energy credits, it has also branched out into other operations.

Of course, these are all just suggestions. There are many more to choose from, especially since the list above focuses on large caps. If you want to find more growth stocks, here's how you can go about it.

1. Figure out what the most powerful long-term trends are

Right now, some of the most promising industries are eCommerce, digital payments, digital advertising, cloud computing, streaming entertainment, electric vehicles, and anything that supports remote work.

2. Identify the companies that are best suited to these trends

While we've given you plenty of behemoths in these categories, there are smaller companies too that have potential.

Maybe they're branching out into different markets, or maybe they're addressing known issues with the large companies. Or maybe they're pioneering an entirely different approach. Very large companies were very small at some point in their evolution.

3. Discover which ones have powerful competitive advantages

Warren Buffett likes companies that have a competitive "moat" around them that new entrants find difficult to cross. For growth stocks, these moats could be in the form of patents or new ways to use technology. Or maybe a company has directors that have education or specific experience in the field that other companies don't.

Network effects, where each new participant makes the network more valuable, contribute to competitive advantage. (Think Facebook.) Having a large scale that allows for maximum efficiency is helpful too, as in the case of Amazon.

Companies that have high switching costs, where it's difficult and/or expensive to switch to a competitor, also have an advantage. As an example, once a business has chosen Shopify for its business, it's unlikely to switch to a different eCommerce platform. (Cable TV providers are also great examples.)

4. Further narrow down to the ones that have large markets within reach

You can use industry and research reports to find out how large a certain industry is, what its growth projections look like, and the companies that own market share. If the field isn't very large and it's not projected to grow much over time, you're better off finding a new investment theme.

You'll want to redo this exercise over time because new technologies are constantly appearing and you'll want to incorporate some of those companies into your list of growth stocks. In the 1980s personal computers, which were all desktops at the time, were a huge and promising trend. Now the trend is computing in the cloud, and computers made a stop at laptops along the way. Expect changes at least every decade and stay on top of the innovations.

DEAL WITH DIVIDENDS

We've mentioned the idea of dividends before, but what exactly are they? When a company has profits, they're often described in terms of EPS, or earnings per share. Those earnings can either be plowed back into the company to help it grow, as in growth stocks or returned to the shareholders in the form of a dividend.

They can be paid out either in cash or in additional shares of the stock, and are generally expressed as the dividend yield.

That's just the amount of the dividend divided by the share price so it's basically a percentage of the company's share price. As long as you held the stock prior to the *ex-dividend date*, you'll receive it. The company's board of directors determines the amount and how often it's paid.

As you learned earlier, growth stocks don't often pay dividends, though some do. There are certain industries where dividend payment is common to most companies, such as utilities, oil and gas companies, banks and other financial institutions, basic materials, healthcare, and pharmaceutical firms.

There are two main reasons why companies pay dividends. One is that it's a reward to loyal shareholders. It helps keep them invested and rewards their trust in the company. The other is that the business doesn't expect to be able to fund future projects that will generate higher returns in the future. Therefore, instead of retaining the earnings for future growth, they pay a dividend.

You may have noticed that some of the industries listed above, such as utilities, oil and gas, and basic materials are all mature industries. These types of companies don't run on innovation like growth stocks, but rather provide services and products that are well-known.

You might also recall from the discussion on defensive stocks that many of them pay dividends. While most defensive stocks are dividend-payers, not all dividend-paying stocks are defensive. Dividends are a signal that the company has strong cash flow and generates profits.

If you prefer mutual funds, including index funds, or ETFs to buying stocks outright, you can find funds that invest exclusively in dividend-paying stocks. Reinvesting your dividends (rather than having them paid out in cash) can greatly increase the value of your portfolio.

Especially in a bear market! Many companies don't like to stop or reduce their dividend stream because that often looks bad to investors. They'll continue to pay even in a bear market, which means that you're getting additional shares of your stocks at bargain prices—without lifting a finger.

On the other hand, if you want to invest in individual dividend-paying stocks, here are some great examples that you might want to consider, screened by NerdWallet.[27]

Name/Ticker Symbol	Dividend Yield (as a Percentage)
ONEOK / OKE	6.26
Universal / UVV	5.25
Lamar Advertising / LAMR	4.75
Philips 66 / PSX	4.36
ALLETE / ALE	4.19
Edison International / EIX	4.13
Omnicom Group / OMC	4.01
Principal Financial Group / PFG	3.82
Spire / SR	3.64
Hasbro / HAS	3.56
Kimberley Clark / KMB	3.52
Bank Of Hawaii / BOH	3.50
Manpower Group / MAN	3.47
Chevron / CVX	3.47
The Clorox Company / CLX	3.33
Eastman Chemical / EMN	3.17
American Electric Power / AEP	3.17
The JM Smucker Company / SJM	3.08
Black Hills / BKH	3.08
The Scott Miracle-Gro Company / SMG	2.97
ONE Gas / OGS	2.92
Calavo Growers / CVGW	2.85
Southwest Gas Holdings / SWX	2.85
Alexandria Real Estate Equities / ARE	2.85
Cummins / CMI	2.84

When choosing your own list of stocks, some of the steps are similar to the process for identifying growth stocks to buy.

1. Screen for dividend-payers

Your trading platform likely has a way to easily filter out any non-dividend payers from your search. There's also a group of companies known as the "dividend aristocrats" (in the S&P 500) that have increased their dividend yield every year they've been in the index. They also might be worth your while to screen.

2. Evaluate the results

You'll want to compare dividend yields among similar stocks, for instance measuring the oil and gas companies against each other. It's also critical to look for the *safety* of the dividend. Is one company's yield much higher than its peers? Red flag. Has it only started paying dividends recently? Red flag. You're searching for companies with a history of consistent dividend payments over time.

Also consider the stock payout ratio, which tells you how much of the business's income is used to pay out dividends. Anything over 80% is a red flag, and if the ratio is 100%, the company may be using debt to pay dividends. Another red flag!

3. Figure out how much you want to buy

Just like all the other investment categories, you want to diversify your dividend payers. How much of your portfolio will you invest in them? How much do you want to buy in the individual industries or categories?

You're better off buying dividend stocks in your retirement or other tax-deferred accounts. Otherwise, the dividends are taxable to you. No matter how you choose to receive them, whether in cash or reinvested, they're taxable.

DON'T FORGET YOUR BONDS

We've been talking mostly about equities and equity funds so far in the book, but when it comes to bear markets, you might want to have some money in bonds. These types of investments are unrelated to the stock market, so they're not affected by a bear. However, they can be affected by a recession.

Bonds are a type of IOU. When it comes to debt that's backed by assets and not, say, credit cards, many Americans are most familiar with a mortgage. You probably can't afford to pay cash for a home that costs hundreds of thousands of dollars. It would take you forever if you had to keep paying rent to save that amount too. Instead, you can save up for a down payment, typically about 20% of the purchase price, and take out a loan (the mortgage) for the remainder.

Suppose you're buying a home that costs $300,000. You have a down payment of $60,000 so the *principal* amount of your mortgage (as always, ignoring taxes and fees) is $240,000. But if the bank gives you this money, they're unable to

DIVERSIFY WITHOUT DISENGAGING | 99

deploy that cash elsewhere for other projects. So although you'll eventually pay them back for the loan amount, they'll charge you an interest rate, usually expressed as an annual number.

You'll pay the interest rate for the life of the loan. Sometimes homeowners accelerate their payments to the bank so they can pay the loan off sooner. Your total loan amount is the principal + interest, so it'll be higher than the $240,000.

How much higher? That depends on the interest rate you're being charged, and that depends largely on your credit score. If you have a high credit score, that shows you're responsible with your money, and you're not at high risk of defaulting on your loan, or not paying it back. You'll have a lower interest rate.

By contrast, if your credit isn't great, you're more of a risk to the bank. They'll charge you a higher interest rate. That way, if you do default, at least they'll have been paid something. When your credit score is really bad, then you're considered a *subprime* borrower.

During the boom that led to the Great Recession, too many mortgage companies were giving loans to subprime borrowers who really would never be able to pay the money back. Because the mortgages kept getting bought by other companies and packaged together, the original issuers weren't on the hook if their borrowers defaulted.

The idea of charging higher interest rates for poorer credit is another illustration of the risk/reward tradeoff. Subprime borrowers are risky, which means you can (theoretically) earn a rich return with a portfolio full of bad borrowers. But you're also at higher risk of losing it all.

In many ways, corporate and government bonds are similar to mortgages. You can't issue a mortgage yourself, but entities can. Bonds are the debt packages of companies and governments. They'll issue a multimillion-dollar bond offering in order to pay for a project or for some other reason.

Typically the government or company issues debt of the principal amount that will mature in a specific period of time and pays the bondholders a "coupon" or "yield".

That's the interest rate that the entity has to pay in order for buyers to hold their debt. And just like the interest rate on your mortgage or credit cards is higher when you have bad credit, so too do the entities issuing bonds have to pay out to the bondholders a higher interest rate if they (essentially) have bad credit.

Individuals have credit scores, but bond rating agencies issue a grade to each institution or government that wants to issue debt. The higher the grade, just like a credit score, the lower the interest rate they have to pay. After all, they have to reward investors for the risk being taken. If they're not risky, then the reward (in terms of an interest rate) is lower.

The US government pays very low-interest rates on its debt, especially on short-term US T-bills, because they're considered very safe. In fact, the yield on the 3-month T-bill is known as the risk-free rate.

When it comes to companies, there are two basic types of grades: a company can be investment grade, which means that it's unlikely to default (be unable to pay back) on their obligations, and so they typically offer debt with a lower interest rate.

Or, the company can be referred to as *high-yield*. Back in the 1980s, these bonds were called junk bonds, because businesses are considered likely to default. Because these firms aren't as sensitive to the movement of interest rates, they actually act more like stocks than bonds.

If a company goes bankrupt or is liquidated, bondholders are first in line to recover some money, or "cents on the dollar". Common stockholders may get nothing.

If you invest in high-yield bonds, you're not getting the cushion from the volatility of the stock market that you do with the other types. The idea behind bonds is to hedge your stock market exposure, so you'll want investment-grade bonds.

Bonds are also different from stocks because they're priced differently. Usually, investors buy bonds because they want the income from the coupon payout. There's an inverse relationship between bond prices and their yields. When interest rates rise, people want bonds with higher yields, so the ones that were already out in the market with lower yields are less attractive. Their prices go down.

Conversely, when interest rates are falling, investors prefer bonds that already have higher interest rates. The demand for these bonds pushes the price higher.

In a bear market, different types of bonds may be better suited for your portfolio.

- US Treasuries

US government bonds run the gamut from 3-month T-bills all the way out to 20-year Treasury bonds. While there is still some risk in all US government debt, right now it's held by investors all over the world. The US government is stable compared to many others and provides more safety than other governments do, as well as more liquidity.

The reason is TINA: there is no alternative. Other governments either can't provide a significant yield or they're too risky. That may change in the future, but for right now, people all over the planet believe that US Treasuries are a pretty safe bet.

They're a good solution for hedging your bets against the stock market, especially during a bear market.

- TIPS/municipal bonds

One of the problems with bonds is that they typically don't provide a good hedge against inflation, especially in a low-interest rate environment. Long-term inflation typically averages 2-3%, and if the interest on your bonds is only a little over 3%, you're going to have a hard time.

Enter TIPS, or Treasury Inflation-Protected Securities. They're US government bonds that are indexed to an inflationary tool so that investors don't experience a decline in purchasing power when inflation hits. As inflation rises, so does the principal amount, and the yield fluctuates with the principal.

Municipal bonds (*munis*), on the other hand, are bonds issued by local governments such as cities and counties to raise money for operations, special projects, and the like. They are also graded according to how likely they are to default.

For both these types of bonds, their performance in a bear market depends mostly on the reason for the bear. For instance, during the Great Recession, there were a lot of fears about whether local governments could weather the storm, so prices dropped.

Similarly, since during the same time assets went through deflation (instead of inflation) with consumer prices dropping due to low demand, TIPS didn't perform well either. But in something like the dot-com crash, without deflation and without worries over local governments, both TIPS and munis can perform just fine.

- Emerging markets debt

US investors often divide the international market into developed and developing (or emerging) economies. You might recall we mentioned the MSCI EAFE index which measures developed international markets—the acronym stands for Europe, Australasia, and the Far East.

EAFE countries are generally considered safer investments, and emerging markets are riskier so they typically pay a higher coupon. You can think of emerging markets as being the government version of high yield. They often don't perform well during a recession or bear market, so they won't provide the hedge against bears that you're looking for.

- High-yield

Similarly, these companies don't hedge your risk well during a bear. They're far more likely to default than anything else.

Sometimes investors get used to the large coupons that these bonds pay out and keep searching for yield. Just remember that high yield means high risk. In other words, when you're getting paid well for taking risks, you should also expect the flip side of the coin: when the markets go down, they're going down too, and they could very well go all the way down to zero.

You might be wondering whether you should invest in bond funds or in actual bonds. Bond funds provide you with diversification, and sometimes perform very well during bear markets because investors are fleeing to safety. (However, they can also decline during bears as well.)

You won't see much fluctuation in prices with individual bonds during a bear market (assuming you're sticking with investment grade.) All bonds start out priced at *par*, which is basically $1,000. Once they mature, they return the principal amount or *face value* to bondholders.

As long as you keep an eye on the type of bonds that you're buying, you can find yourself with an excellent hedge against bear markets and recessions. They're more in demand than stocks are, especially during a recession.

CHAPTER SUMMARY

Diversifying your portfolio in the right way can help you improve your portfolio's performance during a bear market. In terms of stocks, you can look at defensive stocks and other dividend-payers that reliably return income to shareholders. Growth stocks are great during a bear because they're cheap, and give you the opportunity to own assets that are expected to grow faster than inflation. You might also consider owning bonds as a hedge against steep stock market declines. When your portfolio is properly diversified for bear markets, it will perform better even during downturns.

In the next chapter, you'll discover the fifth secret for preparing yourself for a bear market, and that is going short.

6

GET SHORT-Y

While many investors consider going short a tool used by hedge funds and other sophisticated traders, there are a variety of ways in which you can *short* a stock or even an index. When you own a stock or stock fund outright, you're said to be *long* the stock. But when you want to bet against something, you can short it instead and profit from the price dropping.

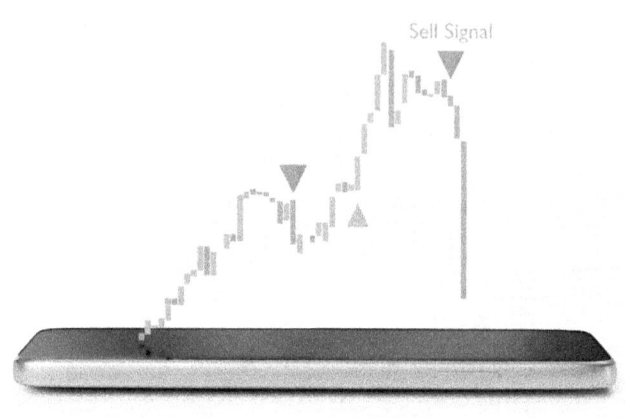

SHORT-SELLING IN A BEAR

You will need to borrow shares for the short-selling technique, and this is known as *leverage*. Suppose you've decided to short-sell the Jekyll company from earlier in the book, with the ticker symbol JKL. It's trading at $50, but you think its price is about to drop. So you borrow 100 shares at $50 and then sell them in the market, generating $5,000 (ignoring taxes and fees, as usual) cash. When JKL falls to $40, you then buy back your 100 shares ($4,000) and return them to the lender. Your profit is $1,000. If you waited until JKL fell to $35, your profit would be $1,500.

As you can probably see, this is a risky strategy. What if you bet wrong? In the example above, if JKL went to $60 instead of dropping to $40, you would actually lose $1,000 on the deal. You generated $5,000, but you have to buy $6,000 of JKL to return the shares to your lender.

That doesn't include the interest you pay while you're borrowing from the lender. For various stocks that are liquid and highly traded, the interest rate may be close to zero. But if the lender believes that the security isn't as liquid, you may be paying higher rates.

In order to sell short, you'll need to open a margin account on your trading platform. You'll need to hold collateral in the form of cash, other stocks, mutual funds, etc., in this account. If you're in losing trades, such as JKl at $60, the platform may make a *margin call* for more collateral in the account to make sure the *maintenance margin* is kept at a certain level.

When prices start dropping, that's when you might fall below the maintenance margin. Depending on your broker, you may have a few days to cough up the cash or extra securities in order to bring it back to the necessary level.

As you can probably tell, you'll need to pay quite a bit of attention to the markets when you're short-selling. You also need to have a strategy for entering trades and for exiting them. On Wall Street, there's a saying: Pigs get greedy, but hogs get slaughtered. For short sales, that means you might want to take your profit off the table rather than wait for the price to fall further.

Going back to JKL that you shorted at $50, suppose it fell to $40 and you'd make the $1,000 profit by exiting the trade (buying back at $40). But maybe you feel that $1,000 isn't really worth your while, and you decide to hold out for $30.

However, instead of dropping farther than $40, it actually bounces back to $52. Now you're at a loss, and if it rises farther you might end up with a margin call. You'd have been better off just taking your $1,000 profit and looking for the next buying opportunity.

That leads to the next question: how exactly do you decide what to short-sell and when? There are three main types of analysis that you can run (you'll learn about more specific strategies as well).

1. Technical

In this analysis, you're looking for patterns in the stock's movement. It can tell you whether the stock looks like it's about to hit a downswing. You will need data on the stock to determine what its typical patterns are.

Once you see it arriving at the lower end of its low price point, but it's still being highly traded, you might consider shorting because it may be about to break that lower price pattern. In contrast, if it's bumping along its higher price range but trading volume is softening, it may be just about ready to start dropping.

2. Fundamental

If you're good at numbers and ratios, you can look at a company's fundamentals (such as P/E ratio) to see if it might be heading for a decline. Some short sellers look for EPS (earnings per share) that are trending downwards with declining sales growth as well, which often indicates a price drop.

3. Thematic

This analysis often takes longer to play out, but you can look for companies in dying industries to bet against. When care came around, buggy whips would have been a great short. The bet against the housing market (as illustrated in the movie *The Big Short*) is a good example of a thematic short as well.

While you do need a strategy for entering the trade and then exiting, it's a great idea to automate how much you could lose from the trade using a *stop order*. This assists you (yet again!) to take the emotion out of it. Stop orders can help you be a greedy pig instead of a slaughtered hog.

But of course, there is a caveat: when trading is at a high volume, your stop order may not come in time to prevent a big loss on your part just because the market's moving so fast. Also, you will pay fees for these orders, so they'll eat into your profits.

4. Buy-stop

This triggers an automatic buy order when the stock price drops to the stop level that you set. For instance, once you shorted JKL at $50 you could set a buy-stop for it at $42. When the price reaches $42, you'll automatically buy back your 100 shares.

5. Trailing buy-stop

Here you set a stop price that trails the stock price at its lows by a certain dollar amount or percentage that you choose. In other words, if the stock rises by that percentage above its low, an automatic buy order is triggered, so you don't lose all your money if you bet wrong.

If the stock falls further below the low by that amount or percentage that you specified, the stop will reset to the lower price.

Let's consider what your strategy for JKL might look like. Maybe it was at $50, dropped to $45, and then rebounded to $52, and you expect it to drop again to $40. You might decide to enter the short when it drops again to $50. You want to limit your losses to $5 a share, so you set a buy-stop order for $55. You decide to exit the trade (close out of it) when JKL hits $40.

Now that you know how to use automatic signals to limit losses, you can try one of these techniques for finding a good candidate for shorting. It's hard to look at stock or industry and "know" whether it's likely to drop in price and thus be a great candidate for short sales. That's why following patterns and trends are so useful. Sure, they can be wrong. But that's why you have a buy-stop in place!

Most technical analysis involves looking at price trends. Generally, an asset fluctuates along its average price as time goes on. The upper limit through which the asset rarely passes, at least when the market is calm, is known as the *resistance* level. The lower limit price is known as the *support* level.

When a stock is on a bull run, it may break through the resistance and start moving along a higher average price point. In a bear market, you'll see the opposite, where it may fall below the support, indicating a lower average price.

- Moving averages

This kind of technical analysis is used very often by day traders. Moving averages shows the asset's average price movement over a specific period of time. The most basic, the simple moving average, is a—you guessed it—simple average of prices by the number of periods in the timeframe you're looking at.

Moving averages analysis can be a bit more complicated than that. There are several different ways to make the older prices less important and more recent prices prioritized.

Either way, the moving average is a trend indicator. When prices are above the moving average, the asset may be overpriced. But if the price remains below the moving average, you can short it while it's still below the trend.

- Sell the rally

Have you ever heard the term "dead cat bounce"? It happens in a bear market when there's a short-lived recovery because investors have moved to *buy the dip*, or cash in on lower prices by going long. However, the rally doesn't last because the bear is still running.

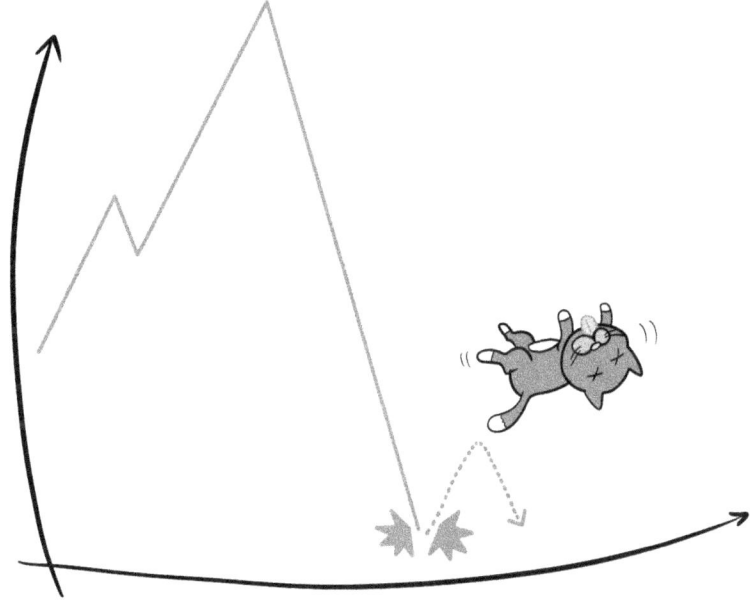

Instead of buying the dip, you can short-sell the rally. Remember that most shorts tend to also be short in duration. The rally on a dead cat bounce won't live long, but if you're watching carefully you can use one of these other techniques to decide when to sell short. Then close out on the thud as the other investors realize that the bear hasn't loosened its grip yet.

- Break and retest

It's pretty common in investing that an asset will be moving along (more or less sideways) and then "break out" either to the upside (bullish) or to the downside (bearish). Then it *retests* at its previous level, and subsequently rises (or drops) again. A day trading strategy that's often used is to go long or buy the asset after it's retested its former levels.

But for a bear market, you want to short it after it retests, because having broken out of its previous pattern, it's likely to fall further. Generally, what happens is that once the price breaks through to the downside, bullish investors will spot its downtrend. They decide to buy the dip, bringing it back up briefly. But as the bear takes over, it starts dropping again.

- Chart it

As they say, a picture is worth a thousand words! Charting illustrates different trends for an asset so you can determine what's going on. Often there are signals that indicate the price will soon start dropping, making the asset a prime candidate for short-selling. There are charts designed just for bearish indicators.

One of these is known as a *bear pennant*. The asset has dropped in price, and after a brief period where prices fluctuate, continues on its downward trend. When you look at the chart, the period of price fluctuation is triangle-shaped and looks like a pennant, hence the name. After the price falls a bit, it rises, then falls again. Subsequent buybacks (where you see the price rising) don't reach the level of the first, so the "high" price is trending downwards also.

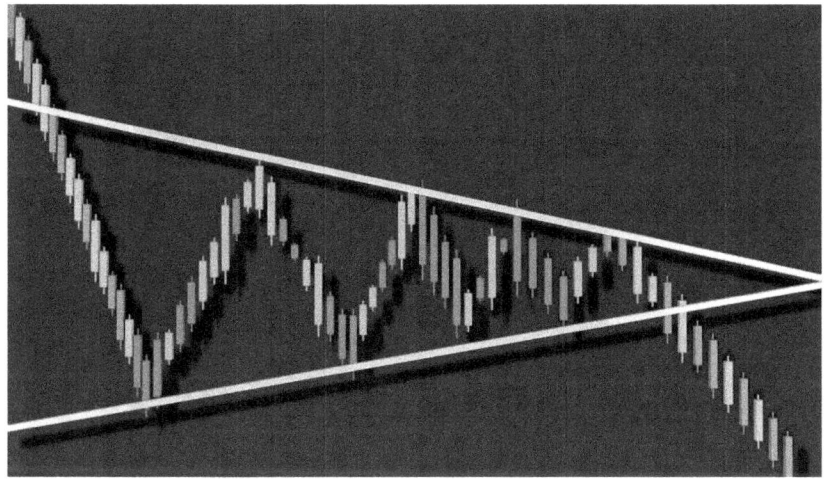

The brief period between the two downward movements (known to day traders as *consolidation*) is the result of buyers deciding that the price isn't low enough yet. Other traders may exit their short sales as the trading volume weakens, and then eventually they're shaken out and the asset continues its price drop. You want to short after the consolidation or pennant formation on the chart.

Another chart is the *bear flag*. This type of chart shows a similar trend, with a downward price movement interrupted by consolidation, followed by another price drop. The difference between the flag and the pennant is that in the flag, the high prices during consolidation are roughly equal to each other. The consolidation period looks more like a rectangle, or flag, compared to the triangle-shaped pennant. Again, the ideal time to short is after the consolidation.

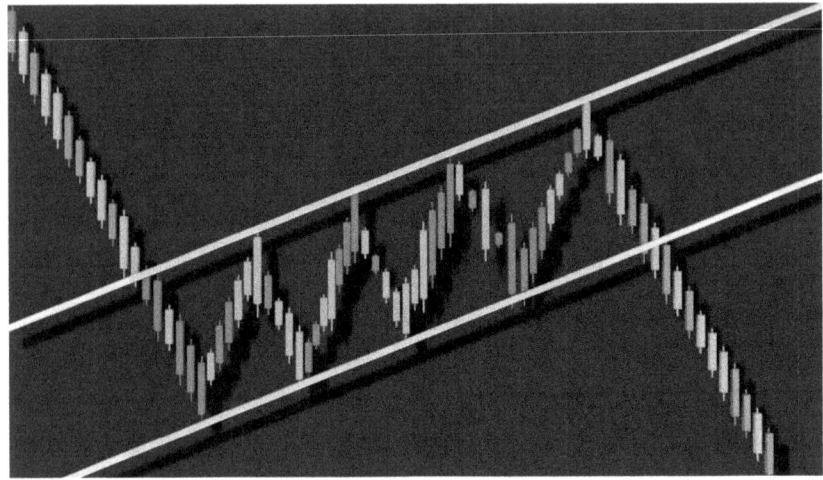

There's also technical analysis that looks at triangles, which are just the shapes made by price trends. You draw one line across the top of the price highs, which in a descending triangle are sloping downwards, as you might imagine from the name. You draw another line along the lower lows or the support line.

Once the price breaks through the support, it's likely to continue to drop or break down, which is your signal to short. You can use the upper line (the resistance) as your buy-stop price.

But if you get short-selling wrong, the risks can be significant. For one thing, your potential loss is unlimited. When you go long stock, the most you could lose is the amount you invested, if the company goes bankrupt or for some other reason the price goes to zero. But in theory, a stock price could keep rising forever, which means you'd keep losing forever. (A stop order of some kind will protect you from unlimited loss.)

As a short seller, you aren't entitled to the dividends that the company you're shorting is paying out. In fact, they could be deducted from your profit to be paid to the owner of the stock. Fortunately, there are a couple of ways to avoid this.

One is to simply ignore dividend-payers when you're looking for short candidates. But that could limit your ability to turn a profit if a dividend payer looks like it's breaking through to the downside. Another trick many short sellers use is to close out before the ex-dividend date. Though of course, that too has its risks, if you'd make a bigger profit by closing out later.

The fees can change on a dime too. Shorting during a bear is often expensive because a lot of people want to short. The cost to borrow a specific stock could jump tomorrow, and so could the interest rate you have to pay on your leverage. Even worse, both those things could happen at the same time.

Finally, if the value of the securities in your portfolio drops below the margin requirement, you'll be subject to a margin call. If you don't bring your account up to the requirements, the brokerage firm may simply close your open positions for you in order to recoup their losses.

In the movie *The Big Short*, you might recall that one of the investors shorted the housing market. The problem was that he thought too many other investors would be trying the same trade, so he got in too early.

The housing market kept rising, so he kept getting margin calls, which was frustrating to his investors as the cost of holding the short kept growing. He told one of the investors that he may have been early, but he wasn't wrong. The investor told him they were the same thing – that being too early was wrong.[28] Eventually, he was proven right, but his investors stopped trusting him well before then.

One last technical term we'll discuss in the short-selling section: the *short squeeze*. Beware! There was a well-publicized short squeeze in 2021 involving GameStop (GME), which is basically a brick-and-mortar company selling games that you can play on various gaming consoles.

Given that brick-and-mortar stores are steadily losing ground to eCommerce, and that many popular games are now played in the cloud, it made sense to short it, and at least one hedge fund did. It's another prime example of a thematic short.

Then, for some unknown reason, the short became known on some internet threads and investors online decided to make a play. Because the stock price was so low anyway, investors start piling in, driving the price up extremely high. That squeezed the shorts, forcing them to exit the trade or lose a lot of money.

Of course, soon thereafter it was clear that GME wasn't worth the absurdly high valuations and its price started to come back down to earth. (GameStop now reports in its 10-K that the stock price is liable to be subject to short squeezes.)

Although in this particular case the reason for the squeeze was essentially a large crowd of online trolls, that isn't always the case. Sometimes you might short a stock and other investors want to buy the dip, or decide that the price is too low for the quality of the company, and the price can soar. Whatever the reason is, it can definitely put you in a bind.

But hey—no risk, no reward. (The guy who shorted the housing market made a ton of money.)

PUT OPTIONS

Puts and calls are options on an asset that gives you as the owner of the option contract the right, but not the obligation, to sell or buy it at a predetermined *strike price*. They're not just for stocks, but can also be used on commodities, currencies, bonds, and indices as well.

The put option is for selling the security, so this is something you might consider in a bear market. You have the right, but not the obligation, to sell the stock when it reaches the strike price, or *exercise* the put.

There are a variety of factors that influence the price of the put. As the stock price falls, the put becomes more valuable. But it's also affected by the strike price, interest rates, volatility, and time decay (as the option gets closer to expiration, it becomes less valuable.)

If the price fluctuation in the stock decreases, or interest rates rise, the time to expiration approaches, or the price of the stock rises, the put option will decrease in value. By contrast, the farther out you are from expiration, or as interest rates and the stock price decline and volatility increase, the put is more valuable.

When you buy a put option on a stock you don't own, it's known as a *naked put*. But if you buy a put option on stock that you own, you've got a *protective put* instead where you can sell your stock. Either way, you're not subject to the same unlimited loss as on a short sale, because in the worst-case scenario the put expires worthless and you're out the premium you paid.

You'll have to pay a premium to buy the put. There's no need to wait until expiration, so if the market is favorable you can exercise at any time. When the stock price is higher than the strike price, the put is out of the money. But once it's lower then it's in the money.

As an example, suppose you're interested in buying a put on Ellemen (ticker LMN). You buy a put option in February that expires in one month. Since LMN is trading at $50, your strike price is $40. Options normally cover 100 shares of the stock, so your premium was $1 per share or $100.

If LMN is trending at $55, your put is out of the money. But suppose it drops to $35 before expiration. Now you're in the money! But remember, you're not obligated to sell LMN.

The value of the put option itself will be around $5, since $40-$35 is $5. Let's say it's trading at $5.10.

You've got a choice: you can exercise your put, or you can sell it. If you exercise, you'll sell at the strike price of $40/share or $4,000 for the 100 shares. Then you buy it back for $35 or $3,500, which gets you $500. If you subtract the money you paid for the put, which was $100, you've got a net profit of $400.

If you owned LMN and bought a protective put, your profit would depend on the price you bought it for because you'd sell at the strike price. So if you bought LMN at $30 and sold at the $40 strike, you'd have a profit of $10 per share or $1,000. Subtract your $1/share premium and your net profit would be $900.

But maybe you don't want to exercise the put and would rather sell it. If it's trading at $5.10 and you bought it for $1, then your profit is $4.10 per share or $410. In fact, most long options (ones that are bought instead of sold) are traded prior to expiration. Not only do you have fewer fees compared to exercising and buying back, but you're also able to capture the time value of the option by selling it prior to expiration when it's in the money.

Conversely, if the price rose, then your put would expire worthless. You'd be out your $100 premium, but no matter how high the price rose, that's your maximum loss (not including fees.) Contrast that with a short sale, where your loss could technically be infinite. Of course, at some point, you'd exit the trade, so it's not really limitless.

You can also write (sell) options, which allows you to collect a profit from the sale in addition to benefiting from a price drop. The risk here is that the rights and obligations are flipped: if you sell a put, then you're obligated to buy back the stock if your buyer requests it.

That means if the stock drops significantly, you might have a big loss. One way around this is to ensure that you sell puts on stocks that you don't mind owning, because that could very likely happen if the stock drops steeply. (This is also a potential strategy for buying stocks you like when the price is low!)

However, if the stock isn't falling in price significantly or it's moving sideways, you'll at least have the premium from selling the put. You may not need to hold the underlying stock if that's not what your buyer chooses.

Some investors like to use put spreads to reduce their risk on a bet that the underlying stock will decline in price. A *bear put spread* is also known as a *debit* or *long* put spread. You use this when you're expecting at least a moderate, if not large, decline in the stock price.

The idea here is to buy put options on the stock you're expecting to decline in price and simultaneously sell the same number of puts on the same asset with the same expiration but a lower strike price. The maximum profit here is the difference between the two strike prices, less the cost of the options.

For instance, let's take LMN trading at $40. You could buy a February put on LMN with a strike price of $45 at a premium of $3.00, so a total cost of $300. You sell a February LMN put for a $1.00 premium at a strike price of $40. Your net cost for the spread is $200.

Suppose LMN drops to $38. Your profit is the difference between the two strike prices x 100 shares; in this case, $500 ($45-$40)x100. Since the cost was $200, your net profit is $300. Worst case scenario, you're out the cost of the spread.

Puts can be very useful, but there's another, simpler way to profit from a bear by shorting. That's by using exchange-traded funds or ETFs.

ETFS FOR BEARS

Exchange-traded funds haven't been around as long as mutual funds (including index funds) and stocks have, and in a way, they're a hybrid of the two. They allow you to buy a "market basket" of securities, rather than buying a stock or bond outright, the same way mutual funds do. However, they're traded continuously on the exchange the same way stocks are, as opposed to mutual funds which trade only once at the end of the day.

They're also more efficient to buy than stocks because there are fewer broker commissions to deal with and they have lower expense ratios than active mutual funds. ETFs can hold commodities and other securities in addition to stocks and bonds. Some mirror particular indices, as is the case with the first ETF known as SPY, for the Spyder S&P 500 ETF. Others track certain industries or sectors, or even specific investment strategies.

Like mutual funds, ETFs can be classified into two main styles, passive and active. Index mutual funds are examples of passive funds. In this style, the managers of the ETF aren't picking and choosing which assets to include in their fund. Instead, they're tracking a certain index or industry or sector, so they invest in all the securities inside that kind of container.

Generally, in both mutual funds and ETFs, the fund isn't actually buying all the securities in the index, but replicating the index in some sort of algorithmic form. Either way, you get the same performance as the index, less a small expense ratio.

By contrast, active ETFs (and mutual funds) have managers that select the underlying securities, which results in a higher expense ratio. Depending on the style and what the managers are tracking, they might be purchasing actual securities or letting the programming do the work.

Below are some of the more common ETFs that you'll find in the marketplace.

- Stock

If you're familiar already with ETFs, you're probably most comfortable with stock ETFs. They often track a particular index, and some investors use these interchangeably with index mutual funds. Like mutual funds, you don't have to stick with US stock "baskets" and can go farther afield with international (foreign securities only) or global ETFs that include both US and international stocks.

You can also invest in ETFs that focus only on small or mid-sized companies, growth-oriented businesses, and dividend payers.

- Industry/sector

These ETFs invest in a specific industry or sector, like renewable energy or automotive stocks. You can also use these to rotate in and out of different sectors during the economic cycle. For instance, you now know that consumer staples are an industry that tends to hold up during bear markets and you might choose to invest in this sector during a bear.

- Bond

Most investors use bond ETFs as a way to generate income. Due to the way they're structured, you don't benefit from the underlying bonds' principal payoffs at maturity. You can find bond index ETFs as well as funds that concentrate only on munis, corporates, government bonds, etc. They also provide a cushion against bear markets just as individual bonds or bond mutual funds do.

- Commodity

Commodity ETFs are a great way to benefit from appreciation in commodities without having to pay the costs associated with owning the actual commodity, whether it's crude oil, gold, lithium, or other materials.

These are also popular during bears because the underlying commodities are often uncorrelated to the stock market. They'll hold up in value even when a bear market has come for stocks.

- Currency

A currency ETF tracks the performance of pairs of currencies, for example, dollars and the euro. It's a good way to hedge against inflation, as well as volatility in currencies for companies involved in importing and exporting.

Speculators like them to bet on price increases, based on what they know about the particular country or region that uses a specific currency. These ETFs can also diversify your portfolio, especially when it comes to a bear market.

- Leveraged

These ETFs are designed to multiply the returns of the underlying investments, typically using derivatives like put and call options or futures to receive 2x or 3x the return. As always, though, remember the risk/return tradeoff! If the underlying investments fall, your holdings could drop by multiples of the underlying return.

- Inverse

These are the ETFs you might think of first in a bear market, because they're designed to short the underlying investments, typically with derivatives. They often come in a slightly different form from ETFs known as ETNs or *exchange-traded notes*, which are essentially bonds backed by an issuer such as a bank that trades like stocks.

You can also find leveraged inverse ETFs, which are designed to multiply the returns you get from shorting through the inverse ETF. If you're expecting an index or sector to fall hard and fast, you might consider the leveraged inverse ETF. But you will need a strong stomach to hold on through dead cat bounces and consolidations before the prices start falling again.

Investing in ETFs is pretty simple. Most trading and investing platforms allow you to buy ETFs, so if you are already on such a platform you're probably set for investing. If not, there are newer ones that are entirely online, or you can go with those that have been around for a while.

Many online brokers allow you to trade without commissions, but that doesn't mean you won't pay for your investment in one way or another. Look into what the hidden costs and fees are, as well as what perks you're being offered, to figure out which one you want to use.

Secondly, you need to research your potential investments. There are actually two viewpoints that you need to take into account when you're determining which ETF(s) you want to buy.

1. Internal

Before you start investing, ask yourself some questions about your strategy to help you narrow down your search. There are a lot of exchange-traded funds that you can invest in, so you need to know exactly what you're looking for.

- Are you investing for growth or income or for some other purpose?

Earlier in the book, you learned about different strategies for facing the bear market. You can invest opportunistically and take advantage of lower prices where it makes sense. You can also hedge against the bear by investing in certain types of investments that perform well during the bear.

You can use a mix of these strategies too. In the next chapter, we'll discuss your plan to navigate bears, and you're probably in a good spot if you mix some of these strategies together.

For example, you might want to include growth stocks and funds in your portfolio permanently and scoop them up at low prices. But you may not always want to invest in consumer staples, so using a sector ETF to rotate in and out could be a good tool for you.

- What's your time frame?

You don't have to rely on ETFs for short-term investing during bear markets. If you like, you can use them for your long-term portfolio as well. But you need to know what your investing time frame is because some ETFs are better suited to the short term and others for the long term.

For instance, given that the stock market grows 8-10% over the long term, you don't want to hold inverse ETFs which benefit from market drops for ten years straight.

- Are there specific themes you already know you want to invest in?

Most of the investment types we discussed earlier, like dividend payers, growth stocks, and bonds are all available in ETFs. One or more of those might have made a lot of sense to you as you read through them.

Or you're interested in tech stocks or financial stocks. Maybe you want to look at what kinds of inverse ETFs are available so you're ready to pounce when you think the time is right.

- How will you invest your money?

Dollar-cost averaging is a good technique for your long-term ETF holdings. If you're planning to rotate in and out of sectors using ETFs, you'll need to plan your entrances and exits.

2. External: the ETF world

After your soul-searching about what you're actually looking for, it's time to find it! By now you probably have an idea about what you want to invest in, and there are some guidelines to help you narrow down your choices.

- Expenses

As you've discovered, active funds typically are more expensive than passive funds. But if you end up with a higher total return, the fee will have been worth it.

- Trading volume

The more the ETF is traded, the easier it will be for you to get in and out of the trade when you want to at the price you want. Liquidity is important because you don't want trades to freeze just when you're trying to sell. If you're comparing similar ETFs to each other, avoid the one that's *thinly traded* and doesn't have much volume.

- Holdings

What are the underlying assets that the ETF holds? Sometimes they'll replicate an index using some algorithms, but others hold the actual asset. Take a peek under the hood.

- Commissions/fees

What are you paying for trades? Many platforms offer ETF trades that are commission-free on both sides (buying and selling). But what is the cost?

- Performance

If you've ever looked at a financial advertisement, you probably saw the following disclaimer: past performance is no guarantee of future returns. That's true, but having said that, very often past performance is an indicator of what you'll get.

If you intend to use the ETF only at certain times, for example buying consumer staples during a bear, then you want to look at the ETF's performance during previous bear markets. Compare apples to apples.

Certain ETFs and strategies can be particularly helpful during a bear market. Kiplinger has provided a list of twelve ETFs that could outperform in a bear market.[29]

These funds use a variety of different strategies to help you profit from price drops. Some of these are titled "low volatility" or *low vol*, and the underlying assets are chosen for their lack of volatility compared to similar investments.

Name/ticker	Type	Assets under Management (AUM)	Dividend yield (if applicable)	Expense ratio
Legg Mason low vol/high dividend / LVHD	Dividend payers	$594.7 million	2.7%	0.27%
iShares Core High Dividend / HDV	Dividend payers	$13.1 billion	3.3%	0.08%
Invesco low vol S&P 500 / SPLV	Equity index	$10.4 billion	2.2%	0.25%
Vanguard Utilities / VPU	Industry/sector	$5.8 billion	2.7%	0.10%
Consumer Staples SPDR / XLP	Industry/sector	$15 billion	2.3%	0.10%
Van Eck Vectors Gold Miners / GDX	Industry/sector	$12.7 billion	1.7%	0.51%
Vanguard short-term bond / BSV	Bond	$39.7 billion	2.9% (coupon)	0.04%
Simplify Interest Rate Hedge / PFIX	Bond hedge	$294.4 million	0.02%	0.50%
Granite Shares Gold / BAR	Commodity	$1 billion	N/A	0.1749%
ProShares Short S&P 500 / SH	Inverse	$2.8 billion	N/A	0.88%
ProShares Decline of Retail Store / EMTY	Inverse (thematic)	$10 million	N/A	0.65%
AdvisorShares Ranger Equity Bear / HDGE	Inverse	$142.9 million	N/A	5.2%

CHAPTER SUMMARY

There are several different ways that you can go short on securities, or even whole industries and sectors, that you believe will decline in a bear market. They range from very risky, such as a short sale where your losses are theoretically unlimited, to less risky, such as put spreads and ETFs. In this chapter, you discovered a variety of methods for opportunistically taking advantage of downward price trends in bear markets. Whatever style of short selling you choose, when done well you'll see solid returns in a bear market as well as a bull.

In the next chapter, you'll learn how to put all these tools together into a toolbox that works for you and your risk tolerance, even when the markets have dropped steeply.

7

PREPPING YOUR BEAR ATTACK TOOLKIT

"Never run from a bear."

— JAIME SAJECKI, BLACK BEAR PROJECT LEADER, VIRGINIA DEPT. OF GAME AND INLAND FISHERIES[30]

Too many investors lose money because they get emotional over a bear market and try to run from it by selling out of the stocks that have declined so severely. Unfortunately, that means they end up locking in their losses. In the past, that might have been you. But now that you've taken the time to educate yourself on the subject, you know what to do instead.

In the past few chapters, you learned about the tools you need to prepare for a bear market and even profit from it. Now you're ready to create your own plan of attack. You've discovered the five secrets to profiting from a steep decline in stocks:

1. Relax and play along
2. Avoid market timing
3. Use dollar-cost averaging
4. Diversify appropriately
5. Sell short

You'll have this book to refer to if you forget any of these strategies or at any time need a little refresher. There is a lot of information here, so don't feel bad if you didn't memorize it all! You may not want to use all the techniques described in the earlier chapters, and that's perfectly fine too. Choose the ones that make sense to you and that you can easily fit into your own life.

While there are specific steps that you can take to create your plan, you also need to avoid getting in your own way. In other words, there's some mind mastery that will help you do the right thing in the face of a bear market.

THE RIGHT MINDSET IS YOUR ALLY

Hopefully, after seeing all the tools that are at your disposal, you're feeling more comfortable with bear markets and more confident in your ability to profit from them. Being able to view bear markets in the right way—as a feature, not a bug, of investing—will help you take the best approach and make some money when others are panicking.

- Accept that bears happen

If you're in a twelve-step group (and even if you're not) you might be familiar with the Serenity Prayer: Grant me the serenity to accept the things I cannot change, the courage to change the things I can, and the wisdom to know the difference.

You can't change the stock market and the billions of trades that occur every single day. No one can. So, there's no hope that you can change the fact that, from time to time, prices will drop at least 20%.

The averages come from long periods of time, and you have to be invested in order to capture those huge days where the market shoots up like a rocket.

The more you can accept that fact, the easier it becomes to look at investing during a bear market rationally. It's going to happen, so instead of denying that you'll ever face one again or trying to hide from it, embrace it and try to make some money from it.

When you accept that bears happen, and even better, start taking steps to capture some profit during a downturn, you'll be making smart choices.

- Avoid emotional decisions

Maybe that seemed easier said than done before you made your way through this book, but hopefully, now you feel confident about your ability to make rational choices. Again, acceptance is your friend, because unless you have a sky-high risk tolerance, you are probably going to start feeling some kind of way when you see your portfolio value dropping day after day.

So don't expect that you will never have an emotional reaction to your portfolio or the financial news again, because that's highly unlikely. What you can do is make sure that you don't make decisions when you're feeling emotional.

There are ways that you can manage your environment so you're less likely to be in a position to make an emotional choice. For one thing, tune out all the blabber from the media (more on that below). Avoid checking your portfolio every day during times of turmoil. Automate your investing so that it happens without you lifting a finger – DCA (dollar-cost averaging) is great for this.

Have a plan so that you know what to do when things get ugly. Is panicking and selling out when you're feeling fearful (an entirely normal reaction, just not a helpful one) part of your plan? No? Then you don't do it.

- Tune out the noise

As noted above, this can help you avoid making emotional decisions. When stocks drop, new channels tend to get very chatty, if not outright shouty. There will be a lot of so-called analysis about *what's going on,* and *how devastating this will be,* and *are you ready for the apocalypse that will surely result from this 20% stock drop,* and so on.

People in the media don't have any more idea than you do about what's going to happen. Unlike you, they have to fill airtime 24/7, and fear and greed are both potent motivators. Plenty of that will be splashed across the headlines.

But they don't know you or your situation, or what your plan is. They're entirely irrelevant to you, and so there's no need for you to pay any attention to them whatsoever. Ignore the financial headlines and news channels. Focus on the research that you've done and the plan that you've put together.

- Maintain a broader perspective

Think about the long-term, not just about what's happening right now. Portfolio losses, even on paper, can be very painful, and part of your brain may be screaming at you to end the pain (typically by selling out entirely).

But when you pull back and look at it from a broader perspective, you'll note that the market always recovers from a bear. Even from the Great Depression and even from the Great Recession. The pain you're feeling during the bear is relatively short-term.

Enjoying a broader viewpoint can also help you profit from the bear. After all, if this is just another part of the market cycle, why not make some money from it? You make money when prices are rising, but why shouldn't you make money when it's falling too? Especially given that periodically it will always fall.

Economies have their ups and downs. The Great Recession was pretty bad, but the economy recovered from it. The US has seen hyperinflation, stagflation, pandemics, recessions, depressions, and wars and still comes out on the other side. Whenever you're in a bear and you're feeling nervous, just remember that this too shall pass.

PRACTICE GOOD HYGIENE FOR YOUR PORTFOLIO

No one knows in advance when a bear market will occur, so periodically updating your portfolio will prevent you from scrambling to get things done when you see a bear approaching. These tips are also good for your nest egg in general, not just when you think the market is about to drop.

- Rebalance regularly

When you don't rebalance back to your target allocation periodically, you end up straying from the risk level that you originally decided would best help you sleep at night during all market cycles. And what feels comfortable during a bull run can suddenly keep you up at night during a bear.

Doing this regularly (especially if you automate it) can help you take the emotion out of it. Because when you rebalance, you're often selling your winners and buying more losers to get back to your target. It's a hard thing to wrap your brain around, so ensuring that you do it every six months or a year, like clockwork, will help you do the right thing for your portfolio.

- Diversify

This is the safest way to handle your lack of a crystal ball. Since you don't know what's about to happen on any given day, week, month, or year, having exposure to different types of assets ensures that you've got some good performers at any given time.

During a bear market, even if every single stock has sunk, you could still have bonds, commodities, apartment REITs, and other noncorrelated assets that are still performing well. When a bear starts scaring investors, they often flee into these alternative classes, driving the price up. Therefore, having some in your portfolio at all times (according to your risk tolerance) will prevent you from having to pay a high price for safe havens.

In the chapter on diversification, you learned about specific stock sectors, like consumer staples, that tend to do well in bear markets. You also discovered that some sectors might be scooped up at bargain prices, which will increase your diversification in the bear.

- Have a "safe bucket"

Some high-quality, short-duration bonds provide a hedge against the stock market drop as well as some liquidity if you need to withdraw from your portfolio. As an example, if you're a retiree living off your nest egg, make sure you have enough bonds to cover you for a few years so that you don't have to sell out of your equities when they're low.

- Keep some cash on hand

Don't buy so much dip that you run out of cash! Leave yourself a little "dry powder" so you can take advantage of future bargains, and also to make sure you don't need to sell anything to meet expenses.

If the bear lasts a year and a half, you still need to eat, have a roof over your head, pay your electric bill, and so on. You'll need cash to make sure you can cover everything.

- Know (and apply) your risk tolerance

If you've never been through a bear, you may find that your risk tolerance is tested. The idea is to know what level of risk you find acceptable, knowing that an investment with terrific returns in a bull run will probably show some significant losses in a bear.

You can dial up your cushion against stock drops appropriately with more bonds, commodities, and other investments that don't move with stocks. Bear in mind that safety comes at a price because you won't enjoy high returns once the decline has run its course.

You can also dial up or down your risk within stocks. There are some low volatility companies where the price doesn't fluctuate very much and you could tilt your stock allocation toward them. You might also consider if you're risk averse, more dividend-paying stocks and sectors like consumer staples that don't fall so hard during a bear.

On the other hand, if you can accept more risk, you might consider tech stocks and emerging markets, which are both highly volatile but have the potential for higher rewards.

Whichever allocation is best for you, it's critical to have it dialed in before the bear hits and prices fall. Which doesn't mean you can't grab some bargains during the bear! But if you'll have difficulty sleeping at night without enough cushion, have it prepared beforehand.

PRIOR PROPER PLANNING (HELPS) PREVENT POOR PERFORMANCE

Life happens, especially in the stock market. You might plan very carefully, and still something could go awry. Having said that, there are actions you can take that will help you ride the bear out and profit from it too.

- Have a plan

This might be the most important piece of advice (next to avoid emotional investing). When – not if – the bear appears in your path, you need to know exactly what you're going to do. Which stocks or sectors will you consider buying once they go on sale?

If you're planning on rotating into sectors like utilities and consumer staples, what is the price point to get in, and what's the exit strategy? Will you be using charts to identify short sale targets? Maybe you have a watchlist for possible put contracts.

Whatever your strategy will be, give yourself specifics for entrances and exits. You might want some stop orders, especially if you're shorting. Know what opportunities you're looking for and generally how you're going to capitalize on them.

- De-leverage

As you've learned, leverage is the use of debt to achieve your goals. Buying a house, a car, or even taking out a loan for a college education is using leverage. (As is a short sale.) Taking out a loan to buy an asset that you wouldn't otherwise have access to is often a pretty smart idea. For example, buying a house with a mortgage allows you to live in the house while you're paying down debt.

However, when a bear market is on the loose, leverage can quickly become a crushing weight on your back. Reducing the amount of debt you have, both in the financial market and in your life, can help you deal with a bear more easily.

You may not be able to pay off your mortgage before the next bear, but maybe you could accelerate some payments toward it. If you have a home equity line of credit (HELOC) and you're able to pay it off, that gives you some maneuverability during a bear because you can access it if necessary.

- Reduce margin

Just as reducing your debt is a good idea before the bear, so is decreasing your margin. You might want to unwind some positions or close out before you end up with margin calls. They can happen very quickly in a bear, especially when it's moving fast.

Protect yourself by taking off anything you don't want during a bear, especially illiquid positions that could be tough to offload once trading gets tighter.

- Create a watch list

Buying the dip is a great way to buy stocks on sale. But you don't want to go to the clearance sale at the department store and end up with too many garments that don't fit or that you won't wear, just because they're on sale.

Similarly, when it comes to buying the dip, you want to have some target stocks in mind. Companies that you'd like to own for the right price, instead of getting excited by low prices and buying businesses that don't help you reach your goals.

CHAPTER SUMMARY

Now that you've explored the book, you're ready to put these tools to use. In addition to the five secrets we revealed, you also need to master your mindset, use good hygiene on your portfolio in good times and bad, and plan for the next bear market. Now you've got the tools your returns can become unstoppable!

A SPECIAL GIFT FOR YOU

A FREE GIFT TO OUR READERS

Are your investment funds underperforming the markets? I share with you four proven steps to manage your fund wealth in a recession.

Diversification through mutual or exchange-traded funds is not enough to protect your portfolio in bear markets and recession conditions.

What if your diversified funds are still performing poorly, how do you know when it's time to ditch your fund or stick along with them? I share with your four practical steps to test on your portfolio TODAY. You can download and start using now!

Scan the QR code below to access your free gift:

https://bit.ly/3DjXQ8D

CONCLUSION

Having read through this book, you're potentially in great shape to prepare for the next bear! You've learned some techniques and strategies that you can use to make money when stock market prices are falling, and can formulate a plan to benefit from a 20% (or more) drop in prices. Although you now have five extra tools, you don't have to use them all if you're not comfortable with them – just use the ones that make sense to you.

Although a bear market may feel quite painful when it's happening, they occur pretty frequently and are a part of the market cycle. Prices can't go up forever, and a bear market can help valuations get back to normal. It's important to accept and move with the bear (relax and play along) rather than fight against it.

You also learned that market timing doesn't work all that well, plus it involves spending a lot of time analyzing what's going on every single day. Simply buying and holding according to your risk tolerance will generate almost the same profits with a lot less work.

Periodically investing the same amount as time goes on, known as dollar-cost averaging, increases the likelihood that you'll sometimes buy on sale. When you automate it, DCA also helps you avoid emotional investing because you'll be buying in no matter what's happening.

If you hadn't already been diversifying before you picked up this book, you now understand how important it is for your nest egg in general. And you can use the principles to maintain some of your portfolio value during the bear (such as buying dividend payers) as well as to buy on sale, for example, growth stocks.

Selling short is another great technique to use during falling markets, and there are several methods that carry different levels of risk. Finally, you discovered how to put it all together and create your own plan.

If you take nothing else away from this book, I hope you feel confident that you can meet the next bear market head-on and even make some money from the stock decline! Now it's time for you to apply what you've learned and create your own bear attack plan.

If you got any benefit from reading the book, please leave a review on Amazon! I would love to spread this message and help other investors like you learn the secrets to handling bears when it comes to finance.

I hope that you did get a lot from it, and I really hope that you have a new-found confidence in yourself that you can use for investing going forward. Best of luck on your investment journey!

Sincerely,

Corns Elba

If you found this book helpful, please spare me two minutes of your time to leave me an honest review on my Amazon page on whether you found this book useful and how you would be putting this content to use.

Many thanks

Corns E

BIBLIOGRAPHY

1. Levy, Adam. "We're Officially in a Bear Market. Here's Why You Should Still Buy Stocks Right Now." *The Motley Fool*, 6 July 2022, www.fool.com/investing/2022/07/06/were-officially-in-a-bear-market-heres-why-you-sho.
2. NBER. "US Business Cycle Expansions and Contractions." *NBER*, www.nber.org/research/data/us-business-cycle-expansions-and-contractions. Accessed 11 Aug. 2022.
3. Ibid.
4. Brock, Catherine. "How Long Will This Bear Market Last? Here's What History Shows." *The Motley Fool*, 22 June 2022, www.fool.com/investing/2022/06/22/how-long-will-bear-market-last-what-history-shows.
5. Carlson, Ben. "How Long Bear Markets Typically Last—and How You Should Think about Investing during This One." *Fortune*, 14 July 2022, fortune.com/2022/07/14/how-long-bear-markets-last-investing-advice.
6. Smith, Anne Kates, and Dan Burrows. "10 Things You Must Know About Bull Markets." *Kiplinger*, 19 Aug. 2020, www.kiplinger.com/investing/600938/bull-markets-10-things-you-must-know.
7. Hartford Funds. "10 Things You Should Know About Bear Markets." *Hartford Funds*, www.hartfordfunds.com/practice-management/client-conversations/managing-volatility/bear-markets.html. Accessed 11 Aug. 2022.
8. Ibid.

9. Anspach, Dana. "U.S. Stock Bear Markets and Their Subsequent Recoveries." *The Balance*, 13 June 2022, www.thebalance.com/u-s-stock-bear-markets-and-their-subsequent-recoveries-2388520.

10. Brock, Catherine. "How Long Will This Bear Market Last? Here's What History Shows." *The Motley Fool*, 22 June 2022, www.fool.com/investing/2022/06/22/how-long-will-bear-market-last-what-history-shows.

11. Investopedia. "How to Avoid Emotional Investing." *Investopedia*, 5 July 2022, www.investopedia.com/articles/basics/10/how-to-avoid-emotional-investing.asp.

12. Investopedia. "Fear and Greed Index Definition." *Investopedia*, 5 June 2022, www.investopedia.com/terms/f/fear-and-greed-index.asp.

13. ---. "How the Power of the Masses Drives the Market." *Investopedia*, 21 Feb. 2022, www.investopedia.com/articles/trading/04/011404.asp.

14. ---. "What Is Market Timing?" *Investopedia*, 1 July 2021, www.investopedia.com/terms/m/markettiming.asp.

15. NYSE. "NYSE Equity Daily Volumes." *NYSE*, www.nyse.com/markets/us-equity-volumes. Accessed 13 Aug. 2022.

16. IRS. "Topic No. 409 Capital Gains and Losses | Internal Revenue Service." *IRS*, www.irs.gov/taxtopics/tc409. Accessed 13 Aug. 2022.

17. Charles Schwab. "Does Market Timing Work?" *Schwab Brokerage*, www.schwab.com/learn/story/does-market-timing-work. Accessed 13 Aug. 2022.

18. Investopedia. "Market Timing Fails As A Money Maker." *Investopedia*, 22 June 2022, www.investopedia.com/articles/trading/07/market_timing.asp.

19. Capital Group. "Time, Not Timing, Is What Matters." *Capital Group*, www.capitalgroup.com/individual/planning/investing-fundamentals/time-not-timing-is-what-matters.html. Accessed 14 Aug. 2022.

20. Merrill Edge. "Focus on Time in the Market, Not Market Timing." *Merrill Edge*, www.merrilledge.com/article/focus-on-time-in-market-not-market-timing. Accessed 14 Aug. 2022.

21. Charles Schwab. "Does Market Timing Work?" *Schwab Brokerage*, www.schwab.com/learn/story/does-market-timing-work. Accessed 14 Aug. 2022.

22. Santoli, Michael. "10 Years Ago This Week, the Market Hit the Climactic Bottom of the Great Recession." *CNBC*, 4 Mar. 2019, www.cnbc.com/2019/03/04/the-10th-anniversary-of-the-climactic-march-2009-market-bottom-arrives-this-week.html.

23. ICI. "401(k) Plan Research: FAQs." *Investment Company Institute*, 11 Oct. 2021, www.ici.org/faqs/faq/401k/faqs_401k.

24. Averkamp, Harold. "What Is Form 10-K? | AccountingCoach." *AccountingCoach.Com*, www.accountingcoach.com/blog/form-10k. Accessed 16 Aug. 2022.

25. Carlson, Ben. "What Should Long-Term Investors Buy During a Bear Market?" *A Wealth of Common Sense*, 7 July 2022, awealthofcommonsense.com/2022/07/what-should-long-term-investors-buy-during-a-bear-market.

26. Gecgil, Tezcan. "7 Defensive Stocks to Buy." *NASDAQ*, 27 June 2022, www.nasdaq.com/articles/7-defensive-stocks-to-buy-for-a-bear-market.

27. Investopedia. "What Is a Growth Stock?" *Investopedia*, 10 Jan. 2022, www.investopedia.com/terms/g/growthstock.asp.

28. O'Shea, Arielle, and Chris Davis. "25 High-Dividend Stocks and How to Invest in Them." *NerdWallet*, 16 Aug. 2022, www.nerdwallet.com/article/investing/how-to-invest-dividend-stocks.

29. IMDb. "The Big Short (2015)." *IMDb*, 21 Jan. 2016, www.imdb.com/title/tt1596363/?ref_=nv_sr_srsg_0.

30. Woodley, Kyle. "The 12 Best ETFs to Battle a Bear Market." *Kiplinger*, 13 June 2022, www.kiplinger.com/investing/etfs/604794/best-etfs-to-battle-a-bear-market.

31. Ewing, LaVonne. "Bear Encounter-Never Run from a Bear/How to Behave." *BearWise*, 30 Mar. 2022, bearwise.org/bear-safety-tips/bear-encounter.

Other references

Baker, Linda. "Tesla's Secret Weapon: Renewable Energy Credits." *FreightWaves*, 25 Jan. 2021, www.freightwaves.com/news/teslas-secret-weapon-renewable-energy-credits.

BehavioralEconomics.com. "Status Quo Bias." *BehavioralEconomics.Com | The BE Hub*, 14 Oct. 2020, www.behavioraleconomics.com/resources/mini-encyclopedia-of-be/status-quo-bias.

Boughton, Noelle. "How Dollar-Cost Averaging Can Mitigate Bear Market Risk." *Wealth Professional*, 14 June 2022, www.wealthprofessional.ca/investments/mutual-funds/how-dollar-cost-averaging-can-mitigate-bear-market-risk/367430.

Business Today. "What Is the Meaning of a Growth Stock?" *Business Today*, 13 July 2009, www.businesstoday.in/magazine/query-corner/story/what-is-the-meaning-of-a-growth-stock-127208-2008-08-20.

Carlson, Ben. "What Should Long-Term Investors Buy During a Bear Market?" *A Wealth of Common Sense*, 7 July 2022, awealthofcommonsense.com/2022/07/what-should-long-term-investors-buy-during-a-bear-market.

Chan, Marcus. "The GameStop Short Squeeze Will Happen Again Because That's How the Market Works | Marcus Chan | DataDrivenInvestor."

Medium, 29 Dec. 2021, medium.datadriveninvestor.com/is-the-gamestop-short-squeeze-inevitable-e395bde8e15e.

Charles Schwab. "Short Selling: The Risks and Rewards." *Schwab Brokerage*, www.schwab.com/learn/story/ins-and-outs-short-selling. Accessed 17 Aug. 2022.

Cherry, Kendra. "How Your Decisions Are Biased by the First Thing You Hear." *Verywell Mind*, 30 Apr. 2020, www.verywellmind.com/what-is-the-anchoring-bias-2795029.

Corporate Finance Institute. "Bear Market." *Corporate Finance Institute*, 27 July 2022, corporatefinanceinstitute.com/resources/knowledge/trading-investing/bear-market.

Daniele, Dttw™. "How to Use and Improve on the Break and Retest Strategy - DTTW™." *Day Trade The World™*, 15 June 2021, www.daytradetheworld.com/trading-blog/break-and-retest-strategy.

---. "Short Selling in a Bear Market with These Handy Strategies." *Day Trade The World™*, 19 Aug. 2022, www.daytradetheworld.com/trading-blog/short-selling-in-bear-market.

Day Trade the World. "How to Master the Best Moving Averages for Day Trading." *Day Trade The World™*, 27 June 2022, www.daytradetheworld.com/trading-blog/moving-averages-guide-on-mastering-mas.

Duggan, Wayne. "How to Prepare For The First Bear Market." *Yahoo Finance*, 10 Mar. 2021, finance.yahoo.com/news/prepare-first-bear-market-trading-172524064.html.

Investopedia. "Defensive Stock." *Investopedia*, 24 Dec. 2020, www.investopedia.com/terms/d/defensivestock.asp.

---. "Descending Triangle." *Investopedia*, 29 Sept. 2021, www.investopedia.com/terms/d/descendingtriangle.asp.

---. "Exchange-Traded Fund (ETF) Explanation With Pros and Cons." *Investopedia*, 26 Feb. 2022, www.investopedia.com/terms/e/etf.asp.

---. "Option Strategies for a Downturn." *Investopedia*, 26 Jan. 2022, www.investopedia.com/articles/optioninvestor/10/options-strategies-down-market.asp.

---. "What Is a Put?" *Investopedia*, 2 Mar. 2022, www.investopedia.com/terms/p/putoption.asp.

---. "What Is an Economic Cycle?" *Investopedia*, 3 Feb. 2022, www.investopedia.com/terms/e/economic-cycle.asp.

Kantrowitz, Mark. "When Dollar Cost Averaging Works And When It Doesn't." *The College Investor*, 22 July 2022, thecollegeinvestor.com/39626/when-dollar-cost-averaging-works-and-when-it-doesnt.

Kennon, Joshua. "Dollar-Cost Averaging Explained." *The Balance*, 29 Oct. 2021, www.thebalance.com/dollar-cost-averaging-356331.

McBride, David. "Dollar Cost Averaging in a Down Market." *David McBride*, www.mcbridefinancial.net//dollar-cost-averaging-in-a-down-market. Accessed 14 Aug. 2022.

Meissner, Fred. "Dollar Cost Averaging in a Bear Market." *Advisor Perspectives*, 17 June 2022, www.advisorperspectives.com/commentaries/2022/06/17/dollar-cost-averaging-in-a-bear-market.

Merrill Lynch. "7 Tips on How to Survive in a Bear Market." *Merrill Lynch*, 30 Mar. 2021, www.ml.com/articles/7-keys-to-getting-through-a-prolonged-market-downturn.html.

Mtetwa, Diane. "Here Are 4 Ways You Can Benefit From Investing in a Bear Market." *The Motley Fool*, 9 Dec. 2020, www.fool.com/investing/2020/12/09/4-ways-you-benefit-from-investing-in-a-bear-market.

Ng, Kay. "Dollar Cost Averaging in a Bear Market." *Yahoo Finance*, 14 June 2022, ca.finance.yahoo.com/news/dollar-cost-averaging-bear-market-181500257.html.

Parkyn, James. "4 Ways to Prepare for the next Bear Market." *PWL Capital*, 22 Feb. 2022, www.pwlcapital.com/4-ways-to-prepare-for-the-next-bear-market.

Royal, James, and Alieza Durana. "Dollar-Cost Averaging: Definition and Examples." *NerdWallet*, 16 Aug. 2022, www.nerdwallet.com/article/investing/dollar-cost-averaging-2.

The Decision Lab. "Loss Aversion." *The Decision Lab*, thedecisionlab.com/biases/loss-aversion. Accessed 15 Aug. 2022.

Thune, Kent. "How to Invest in Bonds and Bond Funds in a Bear Market." *The Balance*, 16 May 2022, www.thebalance.com/what-happens-to-bonds-in-a-stock-bear-market-417053.

Zacharczyk, Ryan. "4 Steps to Prepare for the Next Bear Market." *Dummies*, 26 Mar. 2016, www.dummies.com/article/business-careers-money/personal-finance/investing/general-investing/4-steps-to-prepare-for-the-next-bear-market-192449.

Image Credit: Shutterstock.com

www.ingramcontent.com/pod-product-compliance
Lightning Source LLC
Chambersburg PA
CBHW050418120526
44590CB00015B/2019